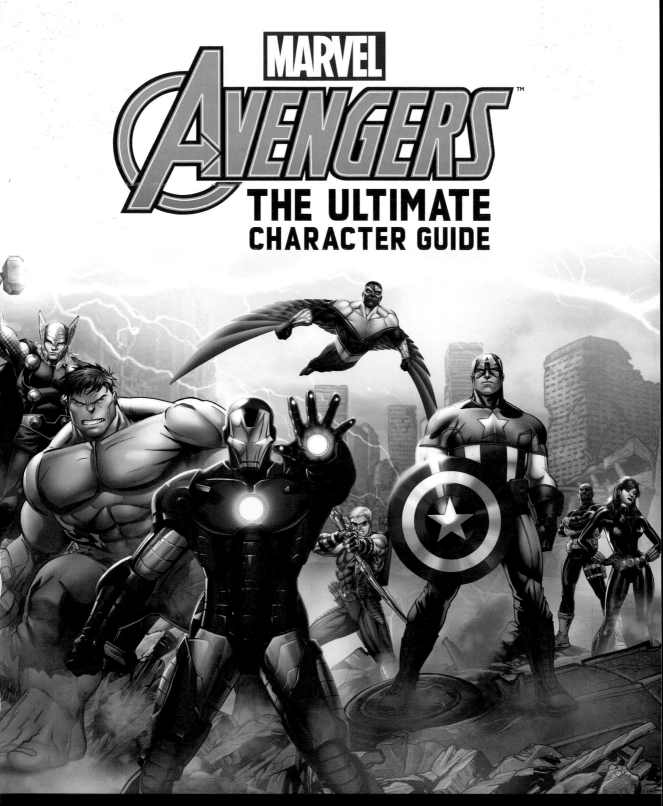

MARVEL
AVENGERS™
THE ULTIMATE
CHARACTER GUIDE

Written by
Alan Cowsill

INTRODUCTION

When Super Heroes team up they are even mightier! Marvel Avengers is the world's premiere Super Hero team, and most of the world's greatest heroes have been on their roster at one time. Learn all about the Avengers, from founding members Iron Man, Thor, Hulk, Ant-Man, and Wasp, to lesser known alumni such as Lionheart, Stature, and Squirrel Girl. Meet the Avengers' deadliest foes, from the evil Loki and Kang the Conqueror, to the more misunderstood villains such as Moonstone.

Contents

This book contains more than 200 heroes and villains with links to the Avengers. Every page is filled with amazing facts and stats, including power rank, for which the top mark is 7. Normal human rank is 1 or 2. The characters are arranged in alphabetical order according to their first names or title. For example, Morgan Le Fay is under "M," and Count Nefaria is under "C." Use the contents list below to zoom straight to each character, and discover amazing facts about the world's greatest team of Super Heroes!

ABOMINATION

Emil Blonsky is the Abomination, a gamma-radiation-spawned monster even more ferocious than the Hulk. Blonsky was originally a spy before using Bruce Banner's equipment to blast himself with gamma rays, mutating into a fearsome creature that Banner's girlfriend Betty Ross called an abomination. The Abomination nearly killed the Hulk in their first battle and has worked alone and with the Hulk's enemies ever since. He has even returned from the dead to attack the Hulk.

The Abomination is one of the Hulk's main enemies and has fought the green- skinned behemoth countless times. His immense strength and power make him one of the Hulk's deadliest foes.

VITAL STATS

REAL NAME Emil Blonsky
OCCUPATION Criminal; former spy; former university professor
BASE Mobile
HEIGHT 6 ft 8 in (2.03 m)
WEIGHT 980 lbs (444.5 kg)
EYES Green **HAIR** None
POWERS The Abomination has superhuman strength, speed, stamina, and durability, and can survive both in outer space and in the ocean depths. He can also slip into an inert state to survive the coldness of space or burial beneath the Earth.
ALLIES Legion Accursed, Rhino, Galaxy Master
FOES Hulk, Avengers, Doc Samson, A-Bomb, Red Hulk

His skin can withstand attack from most bullets and shells.

MURDERED
Another new gamma-spawned creature—the Red Hulk—shot and killed the Abomination, but he was soon back in action.

The Abomination is unable to return to normal human form, unlike the Hulk.

POWER RANK

ENERGY PROJECTION	STRENGTH	DURABILITY	FIGHTING SKILL	INTELLIGENCE	SPEED
1	7	6	2	3	3

ABSORBING MAN

Crusher Creel's abilities not only allow him to absorb the power of objects but also to use that energy to change his size.

Absorbing Man can maintain conscious control even when in liquid or gas form.

Crusher Creel is Absorbing Man, a violent ex-boxer who gained incredible powers when given a potion by Loki, the Asgardian God of Mischief. Loki saw Creel as a pawn to use against his brother, Thor, and in their first meeting, Creel came close to defeating the hero. Creel is a hardened criminal, but he's also found love—marrying fellow Super Villain Titania. Absorbing Man remains one of planet Earth's most dangerous villains.

Creel's ball and chain can also absorb the properties of anything it comes into contact with.

VITAL STATS
REAL NAME Carl "Crusher" Creel
OCCUPATION Criminal
BASE Mobile
HEIGHT 6 ft 4 in (1.90 m), but is variable
WEIGHT 270 lbs (122.5 kg), but is variable
EYES Blue (variable) **HAIR** Bald
POWERS Absorbing Man can absorb anything he comes into contact with. His strength and power increase depending on what he absorbs. He once developed the ability to take over people's minds.
ALLIES Titania, Wrecking Crew, the Stranger
FOES Thor, Avengers, Hulk

THOR'S ARCHENEMY
During Thor's first battle with the Absorbing Man, Thor feared Creel would absorb the power of his hammer, Mjolnir.

ENERGY PROJECTION	STRENGTH	DURABILITY	FIGHTING SKILL	INTELLIGENCE	SPEED
7	7	7	4	2	7

POWER RANK

The mysterious alien known only as Abyss is one of the Gardeners, a collection of aliens who roam the universe seeding worlds to make them better. Together with her brother, Ex Nihilo, she was based on Mars when she first came into contact with the Avengers. While they were originally enemies, Captain Universe made her re-evaluate the human heroes. She eventually joined the Avengers, helping them protect Earth from the titan Thanos and other cosmic foes.

When she first met the Avengers, Abyss used her amazing powers to control the Hulk and make him attack his fellow heroes.

VITAL STATS
REAL NAME Abyss Drusilla
OCCUPATION Hero, avatar of creation
BASE Mobile
HEIGHT Unrevealed
WEIGHT Unrevealed
EYES Black **HAIR** Black
POWERS Abyss' powers remain mysterious. She can control others and function in atmospheres that would kill a human being.
ALLIES Captain Universe, Ex Nihilo, Avengers
FOES The Builders, Thanos

Abyss and her brother Ex Nihilo have created life on Mars.

BATTLING THE GARDENERS
Abyss turned against the Gardeners when they began to destroy planets instead of trying to advance them.

A mysterious engergy surrounds her.

POWER RANK

ENERGY PROJECTION	STRENGTH	DURABILITY	FIGHTING SKILL	INTELLIGENCE	SPEED
4	2	4	2	4	2

A.I.M.

A.I.M. stands for Advanced Idea Mechanics. The organization is led by "Scientist Supreme" Doctor Andrew Forson. Once a branch of Hydra, A.I.M. seeks to use science and technology to overthrow the governments of the world. A.I.M. had three major successes: the creation of the Super-Adaptoid, Cosmic Cube, and M.O.D.O.K. They have even gained their own island nation, nicknamed "A.I.M. Island."

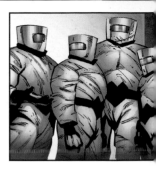

A.I.M. bought the Caribbean island of Barbuda, turning it into their main base of operations—and gaining it nation status in the process.

Superia is a member of A.I.M.'s High Council.

A.I.M. scientists often wear protective uniforms, which also keeps their identies secret. They also employ squads of heavily armed mercenaries to do their dirty work.

VITAL STATS
REAL NAME Advanced Idea Mechanics (A.I.M.)
ROLE Subversive organization
BASE A.I.M. Island
LEADERSHIP Dr. Andrew Forson; previous leaders include the Wizard, M.O.D.O.K., Baron Strucker
POWER A.I.M. scientists operate at the cutting edge of technology—and beyond. Their most notable creations, the Cosmic Cube, M.O.D.O.K., M.O.D.O.M., Minion (Death's Head II), and Super-Adaptoid, have posed major threats to world security.
ALLIES Hydra, H.A.M.M.E.R.
FOES Avengers, S.H.I.E.L.D., Hulk

DEATH'S HEAD
In one reality, Dr. Evelyn Necker created the Minion Cyborg who went on to become the time-traveling bounty hunter Death's Head.

AMADEUS CHO

Amadeus Cho (sometimes known as Mastermind Excello) is one of the smartest people on the planet. His parents and sister were killed by agents of rival genius Pythagoras Dupree when an attempt to murder Cho himself went wrong. Cho's intelligence gets him into trouble as often as it gets him out of it—hardly surprising when he hangs out with the likes of the Incredible Hulk!

Cho persuaded Hercules to help the Hulk during the event known as World War Hulk. Although Hercules was eventually forced to take a stand against the Hulk's rampage, he and Cho became close friends.

VITAL STATS
REAL NAME Amadeus Cho
OCCUPATION Adventurer, former high school student
BASE Mobile
HEIGHT 5 ft 6 in (1.68 m)
WEIGHT 117 lbs (53 kg)
EYES Black **HAIR** Black
POWERS Amadeus Cho has no natural powers, but his exceptional intellect gives him the ability to perform amazing feats. He can deflect a missile attack using a wing mirror, or hack into the most secure computer systems in the world.
ALLIES Hulk, Hercules, Hank Pym
FOES Skrulls, Amatsu-Mikaboshi, Zom (alien monster)

Cho adopted an abandoned coyote pup he found by the roadside.

Nothing about his appearance hints that he is anything other than an ordinary teenager.

GOLDEN MACE
Amadeus Cho inherited Hercules golden mace. Forged by the gods from adamantium, it is virtually indestructible.

POWER RANK	ENERGY PROJECTION	STRENGTH	DURABILITY	FIGHTING SKILL	INTELLIGENCE	SPEED
	1	2	2	2	6	2

ANT-MAN

The third Ant-Man was rogue S.H.I.E.L.D. agent Eric O'Grady. He stole Pym's outfit from a S.H.I.E.L.D. facility and used its powers for his own selfish ends before changing his ways and becoming a Super Hero.

Scott Lang is the second hero to take on the role of Ant-Man, stealing the costume from its creator Hank Pym to try to save his daughter Cassie's life. Like the original Ant-Man, he can shrink in size and control ants. He joined the Avengers and has also been a member of the Fantastic Four and the Future Foundation. He was believed to have been killed during the Scarlet Witch's mental breakdown but was saved by the Young Avengers.

Ant-Man's headgear contains electronic sensors and eye sockets with infra-red boosters.

VITAL STATS
REAL NAME Scott Edward Harris Lang
OCCUPATION Electronics technician, adventurer
BASE New York
HEIGHT 6 ft (1.82 m) normally, but could shrink to any size.
WEIGHT 190 lbs (86.25 kg) normally, but less when he shrinks.
EYES Blue **HAIR** Reddish-blond
POWERS Scott uses Pym Particles (created by the original Ant-Man) to shrink in size while retaining his full strength. His cybernetic helmet enables him to order insects to attack. His wrist gauntlets fire bioelectric blasts.
ALLIES Fantastic Four, Avengers
FOES Taskmaster, Masters of Evil

ANT SIZE
By using Pym Particles, Ant-Man can shrink himself down to any size. He often uses a flying ant for travel.

Ant-Man can communicate with insects and often used them in his missions.

ENERGY PROJECTION	STRENGTH	DURABILITY	FIGHTING SKILL	INTELLIGENCE	SPEED
3	2	2	2	4	2

POWER RANK

ARES

Ares is the Olympian god of war, son of Zeus and Hera. He frequently clashed with his fellow gods, claiming they were growing weak. Ares eventually retired to Earth, but took up arms again to save his son when he was kidnapped by the Japanese god of fear, Amatsu-Mikaboshi. Ares was later killed by the Sentry.

Ares developed a deep hatred for Hercules after his fellow Olympian killed his man-eating birds, which Ares had trained to help him in battle. The two clashed many times, with Hercules often halting Ares' plans for conquering Olympus.

VITAL STATS

REAL NAME Ares
OCCUPATION God of war
BASE Olympus
HEIGHT 6 ft 1 in (1.85 m)
WEIGHT 500 lbs (226.75 kg)
EYES Brown **HAIR** Brown
POWERS Ares has superhuman strength, stamina, agility, reflexes, and durability. Ares is immortal; it is almost impossible to kill him, although magical weapons such as Thor's hammer, Mjolnir, can cause him harm. If wounded, he heals almost instantly.
ALLIES Avengers
FOES Hercules, Amatsu-Mikaboshi

Ares is a vastly experienced warrior, with a deep knowledge of military history.

TEAM PLAYER
After deciding to remain on Earth, Ares joined the Avengers team created by Norman Osborn.

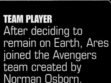

His weapons range from traditional swords and clubs to modern firearms and explosive devices.

POWER RANK

ENERGY PROJECTION	STRENGTH	DURABILITY	FIGHTING SKILL	INTELLIGENCE	SPEED
1	5	6	7	2	2

ARKON

Arkon was a ruler of a barbaric, war-loving kingdom on the planet Polemachus. He believed that by destroying Earth he could kick-start a process that would save Polemachus, which was threatened with annihilation. To this end, he kidnapped the Scarlet Witch and several atomic scientists, hoping to use their skills to save his world. The Avengers rescued them, and also helped save Polemachus from destruction.

Arkon tricked the Scarlet Witch into performing a spell to transport him to Earth, where he would find the scientists he intended to kidnap. He found himself attracted to her, and took her back to Polemachus, too.

Arkon can use his lightning bolts to travel between dimensions.

ALIEN WORLD
Arkon's world of Polemachus mixes high technology with a barbaric code of honor.

His skin is dense enough to withstand high-caliber bullets.

VITAL STATS
REAL NAME Arkon
OCCUPATION Ruler
BASE Polemachus
HEIGHT 6 ft (1.82 m)
WEIGHT 400 lbs (181.5 kg)
EYES Brown **HAIR** Brown
POWERS An expert warrior, Arkon has superhuman strength, stamina, speed, and agility. His skin and bones are denser than a human's, and he heals rapidly. He uses three kinds of energy bolts; the red and black bolts are explosive weapons and the golden bolts open gateways to other dimensions.
ALLIES Thundra, X-Men, Avengers, Fantastic Four
FOES Enchantress, Wrecking Crew

ENERGY PROJECTION	STRENGTH	DURABILITY	FIGHTING SKILL	INTELLIGENCE	SPEED	POWER RANK
3	4	5	6	4	3	

ATTUMA

Attuma was born into a tribe of nomads originally from the underwater world of Atlantis. He grew up savage, violent, and unusually strong, and soon became leader of his tribe. He has fought Prince Namor, the Sub-Mariner, many times and taken the throne of Atlantis from him more than once. Attuma cares about power more than the welfare of his people and will ally himself with anyone to achieve it. He hates the surface world and has made several attempts to invade it.

Attuma has clashed with the Avengers several times. He first met them after capturing the Wasp and holding her prisoner. He did not want her to warn her teammates of his plans to invade the surface world and drown New York under gigantic tidal waves.

VITAL STATS
REAL NAME Attuma
OCCUPATION Chieftain
BASE Atlantic Ocean
HEIGHT 6 ft 8 in (2.03 m)
WEIGHT 410 lbs (186 kg)
EYES Brown **HAIR** Black
POWERS Attuma possesses superhuman strength and the ability to breathe and see clearly underwater. He has been trained in many forms of combat and is an expert warrior fully trained in the use of Atlantean weaponry. He is also faster underwater than most of his fellow Atlanteans.
ALLIES Tiger Shark, Deep Six, Red Ghost, Doctor Doom
FOES Sub-Mariner, Avengers, Fantastic Four, the Sentry

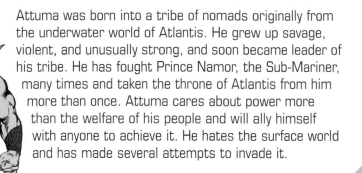

Like all Atlanteans, Attuma depends on water to maintain strength and durability.

Attuma is much stronger than most Atlanteans and can lift 60 tons (54.4 tonnes).

SUDDEN DEATH
During a confrontation with the Sentry, Attuma's head was blasted off. He was later brought back to life by Doctor Doom.

POWER RANK	ENERGY PROJECTION	STRENGTH	DURABILITY	FIGHTING SKILL	INTELLIGENCE	SPEED
	1	2	3	4	2	3

12

BARON STRUCKER

Baron Strucker has forged alliances with a number of fellow Super Villains—including Baron Zemo.

Wolfgang Von Strucker is a founder of the terror organization Hydra. During World War II, he was tasked with stopping Nick Fury and his Howling Commandos, creating his own Blitzkrieg Squad to do so. After the war, Strucker established Hydra as one of the world's deadliest groups. His aging process has been slowed by a special formula. He has also been infected with the Death Spore virus, enabling him to kill with just a touch.

Strucker's scars come from his days as a fencing champion.

Strucker wears a monocle over his scarred right eye, further enhancing his forbidding appearance.

Strucker favors a black uniform—a nod to his Nazi past. He now proudly wears a Hydra armband.

The Death Spore virus infecting Strucker's body will be released on his death, threatening life on Earth.

VITAL STATS
REAL NAME Wolfgang Von Strucker
OCCUPATION Terrorist
BASE Mobile
HEIGHT 6 ft 2 in (1.88 m)
WEIGHT 225 lbs (102.5 kg)
EYES Blue **HAIR** Bald
POWERS Strucker knows several fighting techniques and is a master swordsman and marksman. The Death Spore virus enables him to kill with a touch, slow his aging, and heal from wounds. His Satan Claw gauntlet channels energy and has weapons and teleport technology.
ALLIES Baron Zemo, Red Skull, Hydra
FOES Captain America, the Secret Warriors, Nick Fury Sr.

THIS MEANS WAR
Baron Strucker has been waging war against Nick Fury for decades, first in World War II and then as a Hydra leader.

ENERGY PROJECTION	STRENGTH	DURABILITY	FIGHTING SKILL	INTELLIGENCE	SPEED	POWER RANK
3	3	4	5	4	2	

BARON VON BLITZSCHLAG

Baron Von Blitzschlag was a leading Nazi scientist during World War II but then vanished for many years. When the Superhuman Registration Act was passed, the Baron was put in charge of research for the Initiative. He made several clones of the dead Initiative hero MVP, at least three of whom came to think of him as a father.

Baron Von Blitzschlag can generate limited amounts of electrical energy to defend himself from attack. This power has saved his life several times, most notably against Ragnarok.

VITAL STATS

REAL NAME Werner Von Blitzschlag

OCCUPATION Scientist

BASE Camp Hammond

HEIGHT Unrevealed

WEIGHT Unrevealed

EYES Variable **HAIR** Gray

POWERS Von Blitzschlag was once thought to have no super-powers, but he can in fact generate small amounts of electrical energy. His main source of power is his super-intelligence, and he is widely considered to be a genius.

ALLIES Taskmaster, Scarlet Spider, Henry Peter Gyrich

FOES KIA, Vulturions, Ragnarok, Avengers: Resistance

Von Blitzschlag's ability to absorb electricity has preserved his life and vitality.

SCARLET SPIDERS
Three of Von Blitzschlag's MVP clones formed a team known as the Scarlet Spiders. Only one of them remains alive.

Von Blitzschlag is over 90 years old and sometime uses a walking stick.

POWER RANK	ENERGY PROJECTION	STRENGTH	DURABILITY	FIGHTING SKILL	INTELLIGENCE	SPEED
	3	2	2	2	6	2

BARON ZEMO

The first Baron Zemo was Heinrich Zemo, a Nazi scientist who fought Captain America during World War II. He went insane after his invention, Adhesive X, stuck his mask permanently to his face. When Cap reappeared as part of the Avengers, Zemo formed the Masters of Evil to destroy him. After his death, his son Helmut took on the name and formed a new Masters of Evil. They were later renamed the Thunderbolts, and become a force for good.

The original Baron Zemo fought several battles against Captain America. He sometimes teamed up with his rival Nazi, the Red Skull, to do so.

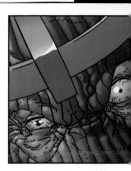

Underneath his helmet, Zemo's face is horribly scarred.

He retains the physique of a much younger man by regularly bathing in Compound X.

VITAL STATS
REAL NAME Helmut Zemo
OCCUPATION Scientist, criminal entrepreneur
BASE Mobile
HEIGHT 5 ft 10 in (1.77 m)
WEIGHT 183 lbs (83 kg)
EYES Blue **HAIR** Blond
POWERS Zemo is a marksman, an expert swordsman, and a gifted scientist and engineer. He sometimes wears circuitry inside his helmet that protects him from psychic assault. He is also able to slow his aging by sporadic immersion in Compound X, a serum he developed himself.
ALLIES Songbird, Moonstone, Atlas
FOES Norman Osborn, Red Skull, Doctor Doom

MANIPULATOR
Helmut Zemo tried to manipulate his fellow Thunderbolts, including a later version of the Swordsman.

ENERGY PROJECTION	STRENGTH	DURABILITY	FIGHTING SKILL	INTELLIGENCE	SPEED	POWER RANK
1	2	2	5	4	2	

BATROC

Batroc, nicknamed "the Leaper," is a flamboyant villain for hire and a master of the French martial art *savate*. Batroc fought in the French Foreign Legion before turning to crime, becoming a prominent smuggler. He also formed the short-lived Batroc's Brigade, a group of mercenaries. Describing himself as the world's greatest mercenary, Batroc is a superb unarmed combatant and has often fought Captain America. However he has rarely posed a serious problem for Cap.

Batroc was hired to attack Wolverine when the X-Man had lost his quick-healing abilities. Batroc's deadly moves came close to killing Logan.

VITAL STATS

REAL NAME Georges Batroc
OCCUPATION Mercenary
BASE Mobile
HEIGHT 6 ft (1.83 m)
WEIGHT 225 lbs (102.5 kg)
EYES Brown **HAIR** Black
POWERS A master of several martial arts, especially *savate*, Batroc is an Olympic-level athlete who can kick through brick walls. He sometimes employs a whip-cane and neural shock boots.
ALLIES The Swordsman (Jacques Duquesne), the Living Laser
FOES Captain America, Daredevil, Wolverine, Sharon Carter, Crossbones

Batroc's boots can emit neural shocks, increasing his kicking power.

KICKING OFF
Batroc's acrobatic fighting style is a result of years of practicing *savate*, a French martial art similar to kick-boxing.

POWER RANK

ENERGY PROJECTION	STRENGTH	DURABILITY	FIGHTING SKILL	INTELLIGENCE	SPEED
2	3	2	6	2	2

BEYONDER

The Beyonder created a planet called Battleworld and brought many of Earth's heroes and villains together to wage war on each other, so he could study humanity's ways.

The Beyonder is one of the most powerful and mysterious beings in existence. Some believe him to be from a universe beyond our own, others the sentient energy from a Cosmic Cube. Intrigued by humanity, the Beyonder visited Earth to learn more about life—while at the same endangering life itself. He later transformed into the female being Kosmos and then the Maker. Following the Maker's death, the Beyonder's energy was again let loose on the universe.

The Beyonder's friendly smile and appearance give little indication of the incredible power he wields.

UNSMASHABLE!
The Beyonder's amazing powers meant even a ferocious assault from the Hulk could not harm him.

The Beyonder based his human forms on aspects of many of the heroes who had fought on Battleworld.

VITAL STATS

REAL NAME Unknown
OCCUPATION Not applicable
BASE Mobile
HEIGHT Variable
WEIGHT Variable
EYES Variable **HAIR** Variable
POWERS The Beyonder can alter reality with just a thought. While he can reshape time and reality, his lack of understanding of sentient life has caused him to do harm. When in the forms Kosmos and the Maker, he became mortal and possessed only a fraction of his original powers.
ALLIES None
FOES No specific foes

ENERGY PROJECTION	STRENGTH	DURABILITY	FIGHTING SKILL	INTELLIGENCE	SPEED	POWER RANK
7	7	7	6	7		

BIG BERTHA

Ashley Crawford is Wisconsin's most famous supermodel. She is also a mutant, able to alter her body fat at will. Ashley helped the West Coast Avengers fight the creature named That Which Endures before joining a team of Super Hero misfits known as the Great Lakes Avengers. They changed their name to the Great Lakes Champions after legal threats from the Avengers.

Big Bertha's alter ego, Ashley Crawford, finances the Great Lakes Champions with the earnings of her jet-setting life as a supermodel. While the team's name may have changed, Ashley's commitment to them has never wavered.

VITAL STATS

REAL NAME Ashley Crawford
OCCUPATION Model, adventurer
BASE Milwaukee, Wisconsin
HEIGHT 6 ft 1 in (1.85 m) as Crawford; 7 ft 4 in (2.23 m) as Big Bertha
WEIGHT 120 lbs (54.5 kg) as Crawford; 750 lbs (340 kg) as Big Bertha
EYES Blue
HAIR Strawberry blonde
POWERS Ashley can increase her bulk to massive proportions, gaining great strength and durability. She can shape her body fat to her will. She is a skilled aircraft pilot.
ALLIES Great Lakes Champions, G.W. Bridge, Thing
FOES Doctor Tannenbaum, Maelstrom, Deadpool

Big Bertha can rapidly generate enough fat to render her body completely bulletproof.

BIG BULK
In her Big Bertha form, Ashley can stop a truck using only her bulk. The upper limits of her strength have yet to be fully tested.

POWER RANK

ENERGY PROJECTION	STRENGTH	DURABILITY	FIGHTING SKILL	INTELLIGENCE	SPEED
4	5	4	4	2	2

BLACK BOLT

Black Bolt is the ruler of the Inhumans, a race of superhuman warriors created by the alien Kree. His voice causes devastating blasts so he remains silent almost all the time, his wife Medusa speaking on his behalf. When Black Bolt felt that humans were coming too close to his home city of Attilan, he once moved it to the blue area of the Moon. He is also a member of the Illuminati. Black Bolt serves his people first, no matter what the cost to himself.

Black Bolt and his brother Maximus destroyed the city of Attilan to save its inhabitants from Thanos. The Inhumans were spread throughout the world with new ones appearing across the Earth.

The fork-shaped antenna allows Black Bolt to focus his powers.

He can harness all of his energy into a single blow, known as the "master punch."

VITAL STATS

REAL NAME Blakagar Boltagon
OCCUPATION Ruler of the Inhumans
BASE Attilan
HEIGHT 6 ft 2 in (1.87 m)
WEIGHT 220 lbs (99.75 kg)
EYES Blue **HAIR** Black
POWERS Black Bolt can unleash great destructive power by using his voice. Even a whisper is dangerous, and, at its maximum level, his voice is as powerful and devastating as a nuclear explosion. As an Inhuman, Black Bolt possesses superhuman speed, strength, reflexes, and durability.
ALLIES Medusa, Gorgon, Karnak, Triton, Fantastic Four
FOES Maximus, Vulcan, Thanos

THE FIGHT GOES ON
After the Skrull invasion of Earth, Black Bolt and the Inhumans took the fight to the stars, attacking the Skrulls, the Kree, and the Shi'ar.

ENERGY PROJECTION	STRENGTH	DURABILITY	FIGHTING SKILL	INTELLIGENCE	SPEED	POWER RANK
5	5	3	4	2	3	

BLACK KNIGHT

One of the first Black Knights created by the wizard Merlin was Sir Percy of Scandia, who fought at King Arthur's side. Nathan Garrett, his descendant, used the power of the Black Knight selfishly and was killed fighting Iron Man. On his deathbed, he begged his nephew Dane Whitman to make the Black Knight a force for good once more. Dane has done so, becoming one of the most trusted Avengers.

The Black Knight has been part of many teams, including the Avengers, but was most recently a member of the British Super Hero group MI-13. As part of that team he helped to prevent a vampire invasion of the U.K. led by Dracula.

VITAL STATS

REAL NAME Dane Whitman
OCCUPATION Scientist, adventurer
BASE Garrett Castle
HEIGHT 6 ft (1.82 m)
WEIGHT 190 lbs (86.25 kg)
EYES Brown **HAIR** Brown
POWERS The Black Knight is a superb swordsman. He is armed with the Ebony Blade, a sword forged by Merlin in the time of King Arthur. It can cut through any substance but also carries a curse—if its wielder uses it in an unworthy manner, the sword will drive them insane.
ALLIES Crystal, Sersi, Doctor Strange, Captain Britain
FOES Bloodwraith, Morgan Le Fay

The Ebony Blade can cut through any substance, and deflect, pierce, or absorb energy blasts.

FINDING A SQUIRE
While fighting with MI-13, Dane met and fell in love with Faiza Hussain, whom he took on as his squire.

POWER RANK

ENERGY PROJECTION	STRENGTH	DURABILITY	FIGHTING SKILL	INTELLIGENCE	SPEED
4	2	5	5	4	2

BLACK PANTHER

The Black Panther is a title given to the ruler of the African nation of Wakanda. In modern times, T'Challa was the Black Panther and took on the powers that go with the role. He traveled to America to see if the Super Heroes there could be a threat to his homeland but soon became allies with many of them, joining the Avengers and briefly marrying Storm of the X-Men. His sister, Shuri, now rules Wakanda, T'Challa acting as her second.

Black Panther took over the role of protector of Hell's Kitchen in New York from Daredevil. He assumed the identity of Mr. Okonkwo, opening a diner called Devil's Kitchen. This front allowed him to test his abilities as Black Panther against New York's toughest criminals.

SHURI
When T'Challa was injured, his sister Shuri took on the role of Black Panther and continues to rule Wakanda.

Cloaking technology in his costume can make it appear to be normal street clothing.

Energy daggers and metal-dissolving claws are concealed in his gloves.

Vibranium pads on his boot soles allow him to walk on water, climb walls, and tread silently.

VITAL STATS
REAL NAME T'Challa
OCCUPATION Adventurer, former king
BASE Wakanda
HEIGHT 6 ft (1.82 m)
WEIGHT 200 lbs (90.75 kg)
EYES Brown **HAIR** Black
POWERS T'Challa's senses and athleticism are enhanced by mystical herbs that only a Black Panther may use. His suit contains the metal Vibranium which absorbs impact, making him bulletproof. His hands and feet have Vibranium pads that allow him to climb walls with ease. He is also an expert warrior.
ALLIES Fantastic Four, Avengers, Illuminati
FOES Magneto, Doctor Doom, Man-Ape, Klaw

ENERGY PROJECTION	STRENGTH	DURABILITY	FIGHTING SKILL	INTELLIGENCE	SPEED	POWER RANK
3	3	3	5	5		

BLACK WIDOW

Natalia Romanova (a.k.a. Natasha Romanova) was one of the Soviet Union's top spies. She was codenamed the Black Widow and sent to the U.S.A. to spy on Tony Stark's (Iron Man's) company, but met Hawkeye, who convinced her to leave her Soviet masters. She has since worked with S.H.I.E.L.D. and the Avengers and was a member of the Champions of Los Angeles.

Since leaving the old Soviet Union, the Black Widow has worked with S.H.I.E.L.D. on many missions. She has often teamed up with Captain America, who saved her life when she was a child.

VITAL STATS

REAL NAME Natalia "Natasha" Alianovna Romanova
OCCUPATION Spy, former ballerina
BASE Mobile
HEIGHT 5 ft 7 in (1.70 m)
WEIGHT 125 lbs (57 kg)
EYES Blue **HAIR** Red/auburn
POWERS A version of the Super Soldier Serum keeps the Black Widow in peak condition. Her bracelets contain the "widow's line" (a cable used for swinging and climbing) and the "widow's bite," which fires electric bolts. Her belt carries explosives.
ALLIES Hawkeye, Nick Fury, Iron Man, Wolverine, Captain America
FOES Hydra, Black Widow (Yelena Belova), Baron Strucker

Her wrist gauntlets fire electric bolts to stun opponents.

ATHLETICISM
The Black Widow is a fully trained ballerina as well as a spy. Her athletic prowess has saved her life countless times.

The Black Widow's aging process has been slowed by a modified Super Soldier Serum.

POWER RANK

ENERGY PROJECTION	STRENGTH	DURABILITY	FIGHTING SKILL	INTELLIGENCE	SPEED
3	3	3	6	3	2

BLACKOUT

An accident gave lab assistant Marcus Daniels the power to control energy from the Darkforce dimension. He used this ability to attack those he felt had wronged him and to begin a life of crime. The Darkforce energy made Marcus mentally unstable and he was manipulated by other villains, including Baron Zemo and Moonstone. He recovered from a clash with Zemo to join the Hood's criminal gang.

The first Super Hero to fight Blackout was Nova. Blackout nearly booted the young hero but, following his defeat, the villain found himself trapped in the Darkforce dimension.

Exposure to the Darkforce energy soon drove Blackout insane.

Blackout can project Darkforce energy with great concussive force.

VITAL STATS

REAL NAME Marcus Daniels
OCCUPATION Criminal
BASE Mobile
HEIGHT 5 ft 10 in (1.78 m)
WEIGHT 180 lbs (81.75 kg)
EYES Gray **HAIR** Brown
POWERS Blackout can manipulate energy from the Darkforce dimension (a dimension filled with strange dark matter). He can manipulate this energy into any shape. He can also open gateways to the Darkforce dimension and transport people there.
ALLIES Baron Zemo, Moonstone, Thunderbolts, the Hood
FOES Nova, Avengers, Dazzler, Quicksilver

SIEGE
Blackout was used by Zemo to attack the Avengers. Blackout cut the Avengers Mansion off from the world with Darkforce energy.

ENERGY PROJECTION	STRENGTH	DURABILITY	FIGHTING SKILL	INTELLIGENCE	SPEED
5	2	6	2	2	7

POWER RANK

BLADE

Eric Brooks was born a vampire-human hybrid due to a bloodsucker called Deacon Frost feasting on his mother. He has dedicated his life to hunting vampires and other demonic creatures. The nature of his parentage led to vampire enzymes entering his bloodstream, making him immune to most vampire bites. An attack by Morbius the Living Vampire left Blade with exceptional strength. Alongside Luke Cage's Mighty Avengers, Blade took on the role of Ronin to track down the Deathwalkers cult.

Blade fought alongside Captain Britain and the heroes of MI-13 when Dracula and an army of vampires tried to invade the U.K. He still has close ties to his old allies.

VITAL STATS

REAL NAME Eric Brooks
OCCUPATION Vampire hunter
BASE Mobile
HEIGHT 6 ft 2 in (1.87 m)
WEIGHT 215 lbs (97.5 kg)
EYES Brown **HAIR** Black
POWERS Vampire enzymes in Blade's blood have slowed his aging. Blade also has superhuman speed, strength, and a bloodlust, earning him the name "Daywalker" (a half-vampire who works in sunlight). Blade is trained in martial arts and maintains peak physical condition.
ALLIES Captain Britain, Doctor Strange, Spider-Man, Luke Cage, Spectrum
FOES Dracula, Deacon Frost, all vampires

Vampire infection has left Blade with sharp fangs.

Blade is expert with all bladed weapons, particularly swords.

OLD SCHOOL
In the 1970s, Blade (on right) fought alongside Luke Cage's father, James Lucas, a New York City cop.

	ENERGY PROJECTION	STRENGTH	DURABILITY	FIGHTING SKILL	INTELLIGENCE	SPEED
POWER RANK	1	4	4	5	2	2

BLOODWRAITH

Sean Dolan was an orphan taken in by the Black Knight (Dane Whitman) to be trained as his squire. However, when Dolan used the Black Knight's Ebony Blade, the sword's curse changed him into the vicious Bloodwraith, the blade urging him on to kill more and more innocent people. During his last outing, it took the combined might of the entire Avengers team to stop Bloodwraith.

Bloodwraith became almost unstoppable after claiming the souls of Slorenians killed during Ultron's massacre. The Avengers could only contain him by trapping him permanently in Slorenia.

The Ebony Blade can slice through any material and is thought to be indestructible.

FRIEND BECOMES FOE
Once a loyal squire, Bloodwraith became the archenemy of his old mentor, the Black Knight.

The power from the souls taken by the sword casts a mystical glow around Bloodwraith.

REAL NAME Sean Dolan
OCCUPATION Super Villain
BASE Mobile
HEIGHT 5 ft 11 in (1.80 m) as Dolan; 100 ft (30.48 m) as Bloodwraith
WEIGHT 160 lbs (72.59 kg) as Dolan; unrevealed as Bloodwraith
EYES Blue (as Dolan); red, later white (as Bloodwraith)
HAIR Reddish blond (as Dolan); none (as Bloodwraith)
POWERS Bloodwraith has superhuman strength and speed. When the Ebony Blade took many souls, he grew to giant size, with even greater strength and durability.
ALLIES None
FOES Black Knight, Avengers, Doctor Strange

ENERGY PROJECTION	STRENGTH	DURABILITY	FIGHTING SKILL	INTELLIGENCE	SPEED	POWER RANK
1	4	3	5	2	2	

B

25

BLUE MARVEL

Adam Brashear is a veteran of the Korean War and one of the world's most powerful Super Heroes. He was working on a method of harnessing energy from the Negative Zone when an explosion mutated him, giving him exceptional powers and effectively making him an antimatter reactor. He became the Blue Marvel, but soon retired. He later returned to active duty to help Luke Cage's Avengers take on Thanos' forces and decided to remain as part of the team.

Adam had a long friendship with Uatu the Watcher. Following Uatu's assassination, Adam learned that his old friend wished him to be the godfather of his unborn child.

VITAL STATS

REAL NAME Adam Brashear
OCCUPATION Scientist and Super Hero
BASE Kadesh (underwater headquarters situated in the Marianas Trench)
HEIGHT 6 ft 4 in (1.93 m)
WEIGHT 230 lbs (104.25 kg)
EYES Brown
HAIR Black (with gray highlights)
POWERS Superhuman strength, speed, senses, and agility. Adam can also fly and survive in space, The true extent of his powers is yet to be revealed.
ALLIES Mighty Avengers, Reed Richards, Uatu the Watcher
FOES Anti-Man, Shuma-Gorath

Adam Brashear is one of the most brilliant scientists in the world.

Adam's body is an antimatter reactor, giving him almost limitless power.

BAD APPLE
Adam's oldest son, Kevin, became the mad scientist known as Dr. Positron.

POWER RANK

ENERGY PROJECTION	STRENGTH	DURABILITY	FIGHTING SKILL	INTELLIGENCE	SPEED
5	7	6	4	6	5

BULLSEYE

Bullseye is one of the deadliest assassins in the world, and specializes in throwing objects. He is Daredevil's archenemy, and his victims include two people close to Daredevil—Elektra and Karen Page. Bullseye was paralyzed during a fight with Daredevil but his body was repaired by Japanese scientist Lord Dark Wind, who laced Bullseye's bones with Adamantium. Bullseye joined Norman Osborn's Thunderbolts group and later his Avengers team.

Bullseye disguised himself as Hawkeye when he was in Norman Osborn's Avengers team. Osborn also used him as his own personal assassin, ordering him to kill the Sentry's wife, Lindy Reynolds.

WEAPONS ACE
Bullseye killed Elektra using her own sai and a playing card. He claims that, in his hands, anything can become a deadly weapon.

His skeleton is laced with Adamantium, the strongest metal known to man.

He can throw objects with equal accuracy from either hand.

VITAL STATS

REAL NAME Lester (last name unknown)
OCCUPATION Assassin
BASE Mobile
HEIGHT 6 ft (1.82 m)
WEIGHT 200 lbs (90.75 kg) including Adamantium implants; previous weight 175 lbs (79.25 kg)
EYES Blue **HAIR** Blond
POWERS Bullseye's ability to hit a target is almost superhuman. He is an expert martial artist and a highly trained weapons expert. The Adamantium laced to his skeleton not only protects him from harm, but helps him perform acrobatic feats.
ALLIES Kingpin, Norman Osborn
FOES Daredevil, Elektra, Punisher

ENERGY PROJECTION	STRENGTH	DURABILITY	FIGHTING SKILL	INTELLIGENCE	SPEED	POWER RANK
1	2	3	5	2	2	

CAPTAIN AMERICA

Student Steve Rogers was deemed too weedy to fight in World War II. He agreed to take part in a top-secret experiment and emerged as a Super Soldier—Captain America! Cap fought alongside the army until the last days of the war, when an accident left him frozen in ice until he was found by the Avengers. Since then, Cap's strength, dignity, and battle skills have made him one of the world's greatest Super Heroes.

During a time when he wasn't Captain America, Steve Rogers formed a covert group of Super Heroes known as the Secret Avengers.

VITAL STATS
REAL NAME Steve Rogers
OCCUPATION Adventurer, S.H.I.E.L.D. operative
BASE New York
HEIGHT 6 ft 2 in (1.87 m)
WEIGHT 220 lbs (99.75 kg)
EYES Blue **HAIR** Blond
POWERS Captain America is the pinnacle of human physical perfection. He is an expert boxer and highly trained in judo and many other martial arts. The Super Soldier Serum has also given him superhuman powers of endurance.
ALLIES Sharon Carter, Iron Man, Sub-Mariner, Bucky Barnes, Falcon, Thor
FOES Red Skull, Baron Zemo, Sin

Cap's shield is made of a Vibranium composite and is virtually indestructible.

The Super Soldier Serum made Steve Rogers the peak of physical perfection.

THE NEW CAPTAIN AMERICA
Sam Wilson (the Falcon) took over as Captain America when age caught up with Steve Rogers.

POWER RANK	ENERGY PROJECTION	STRENGTH	DURABILITY	FIGHTING SKILL	INTELLIGENCE	SPEED
	1	3	3	6	3	2

CAPTAIN BRITAIN

Brian Braddock is Captain Britain, the U.K.'s greatest hero and the guardian of the Omniverse. Captain Britain has protected his homeland from a multitude of threats. He's the twin brother of Psylocke, and has worked as an agent of MI-13 and S.H.I.E.L.D.'s European division. As a member of the Secret Avengers, he battled a robotic race called the Descendants. He also established the Braddock Academy to train the U.K.'s young heroes.

Captain Britain was asked by Captain America Steve Rogers to join a covert group named the Secret Avengers. Captain Britain's powerful skills proved an asset to the team as they faced the threat of the machine-like Descendants.

STANDING TOGETHER
Captain Britain fought alongside Death's Head II, Dark Angel, and other U.K.-based heroes when Killpower returned from Hell.

Captain Britain's Union Flag costume reflects his role as the U.K.'s protector.

His costume once functioned as a battery, storing multidimensional energies and giving him super-powers, but now has no special properties.

VITAL STATS
REAL NAME Brian Braddock
OCCUPATION Adventurer
BASE Braddock Manor
HEIGHT 6 ft 6 in (1.98 in)
WEIGHT 257 lbs (116.57 kg)
EYES Blue **HAIR** Blond
POWERS Captain Britain can fly at supersonic speeds and has superhuman strength and reflexes. Since he was brought back to life by the wizard Merlin, his powers stem from magic and are linked to his own self-confidence. He is also less susceptible to telepathic attack since his rebirth.
ALLIES Black Knight, Psylocke, Meggan, X-Men, Avengers
FOES Mad Jim Jaspers, The Fury, Killpower

ENERGY PROJECTION	STRENGTH	DURABILITY	FIGHTING SKILL	INTELLIGENCE	SPEED	POWER RANK
3	6	6	4	5	4	

CAPTAIN MARVEL (DANVERS)

Carol Danvers is Captain Marvel, one of the world's greatest Super Heroes and a popular member of the Avengers. She gained her powers after meeting the original Captain Mar-Vell (an alien Kree hero) and getting caught in a Kree Psyche-Magnitron, which altered her genetic structure, making her a human-Kree hybrid. At first, Carol took the codename Ms. Marvel; she has also been known as Binary and Warbird.

Carol's archenemy Moonstone took on the role of Ms. Marvel in Norman Osborn's Avengers, leading to a violent confrontation between Carol and her rival.

VITAL STATS
REAL NAME Carol Susan Jane Danvers
OCCUPATION Adventurer, former N.A.S.A. security chief
BASE Mobile
HEIGHT 5 ft 11 in (1.80 m)
WEIGHT 124 lbs (56.25 kg)
EYES Blue **HAIR** Blonde
POWERS Captain Marvel can fly at incredible speeds and has amazing strength and durability. She can fire photonic blasts and absorb energy.
ALLIES Iron Man, Iron Patriot, Starjammers, Guardians of the Galaxy
FOES Yon-Rogg, Moonstone, M.O.D.O.K., Absorbing Man

Captain Marvel has a "seventh sense" that helps her anticipate opponents' attacks.

Captain Marvel's body absorbs energy and is bulletproof.

Captain America suggested Carol take on the mantle of Captain Marvel to honor the memory of the original Kree hero Mar-Vell.

BINARY
If Carol's body absorbs enough energy, she can return to Binary form, capable of channeling virtually unlimited cosmic power.

POWER RANK	ENERGY PROJECTION	STRENGTH	DURABILITY	FIGHTING SKILL	INTELLIGENCE	SPEED
	5	5	6	4	3	5

CAPTAIN MARVEL (MAR-VELL)

Mar-Vell was a Kree warrior sent to Earth to sabotage humanity's space program. However he grew to admire humans and started to help them, gaining the title Captain Marvel while fighting such foes as Thanos and the Skrulls. Sadly, Mar-Vell developed cancer after fighting the villain Nitro, and died. Others—including his own son Genis-Vell—have tried to take on his title. The latest hero to take on his heroic legacy is Carol Danvers.

Captain Marvel once returned to action after being found in the Negative Zone. He was later revealed to be a Skrull called Khn'nr. However, Khn'nr believed he was Captain Marvel and died defending the Earth from his fellow Skrulls.

Cosmic awareness alerted Captain Marvel to enemy weaknesses and allowed him to see the future.

The Nega-Bands stored solar energy, converting it into photon blasts.

VITAL STATS
REAL NAME Mar-Vell
OCCUPATION Former captain in the Kree space fleet
BASE Mobile
HEIGHT 6 ft 2 in (1.87 m)
WEIGHT 240 lbs (108.75 kg)
EYES Blue **HAIR** Blond
POWERS Mar-Vell used solar energy, stored in Nega-Bands worn on his wrists, to gain superhuman strength, speed, energy blasts, and the power of flight. He also had cosmic awareness, which enabled him to pinpoint an enemy's weakness.
ALLIES Rick Jones, Avengers, Silver Surfer, Adam Warlock, Starfox, Mr. Fantastic
FOES Thanos, Nitro, Super Skrull, Zarek, Ronan

BONDING
Captain Marvel was once bonded to Rick Jones. Rick summoned Marvel to take his place via the Nega-Bands.

ENERGY PROJECTION	STRENGTH	DURABILITY	FIGHTING SKILL	INTELLIGENCE	SPEED	POWER RANK
5	4	3	4	3	7	

CAPTAIN UNIVERSE

Captain Universe is the title given to individuals possessed by a mysterious cosmic force of near-limitless energy. This force possesses people at times of crisis and endows them with various cosmic powers. It possessed comatose car-crash victim Tamara Devoux when the Earth was threatened. As the new Captain Universe, she became a member of the Avengers and helped the team to bring Ex Nihilo and Abyss into its ranks.

Tamara Devoux was in a coma when the cosmic force selected her to be its host. It did so because it too was broken and dying like Tamara.

VITAL STATS

REAL NAME Tamara Devoux
OCCUPATION Adventurer
BASE Stark Tower, New York City
HEIGHT Unrevealed
WEIGHT Unrevealed
EYES White **HAIR** None
POWERS The cosmic force grants near-limitless power, flight, and superhuman strength. The extent of the power is sometimes limited by the host. While possessing Tamara, the force was "broken"—like its comatose host.
ALLIES Avengers, Spider-Man, Star-Lord, Shang-Chi
FOES Psycho-Man, Ultron, Aleph

The costume reflects the molecular changes the cosmic force brings to its host, granting the host amazing abilities.

The Captain Universe costume adapts to its host's body and protects against extreme temperatures.

CITY SAVIOR
Spider-Man met a native New Yorker who had become Captain Universe to save the city from destruction.

POWER RANK	ENERGY PROJECTION	STRENGTH	DURABILITY	FIGHTING SKILL	INTELLIGENCE	SPEED
	7	2	2	1	7	5

CHARLIE-27

In the 31st century, Charlie-27 was one of a race of genetically-engineered humans sent to live on the harsh planet of Jupiter. While he was away on a solo space mission, evil aliens the Badoon wiped out everyone on the planet. Charlie-27 became a freedom fighter, joining the Guardians of the Galaxy to fight and defeat the Badoon invaders. He has also traveled back in time to fight alongside the Avengers in the present day.

When Charlie-27 traveled back to the present, he clashed with Beast and his fellow Avengers. However, the two groups eventually teamed up.

PILOT CHARLIE
Charlie-27 has piloted several ships for the Guardians of the Galaxy, including two named after Captain America.

Charlie-27's large, heavy body allows him to withstand Jupiter's strong gravity.

Charlie-27's costume is typical of many worn by Jupiter's pre-Badoon invasion settlers.

VITAL STATS
REAL NAME Charlie-27
OCCUPATION Adventurer
BASE Mobile
HEIGHT 6 ft (1.82 m)
WEIGHT 555 lbs (251.75 kg)
EYES Blue **HAIR** Red
POWERS Charlie-27 is one of a race of humans who were genetically adapted to live on Jupiter, possessing superhuman strength, stamina, and durability. A militia-man highly trained in hand-to-hand combat, Charlie-27 is also a skilled pilot, able to control most 31st-century spacecraft.
ALLIES Avengers, Guardians of the Galaxy, Silver Surfer, Talon, Yellowjacket, Hollywood, Thor
FOES Badoon, Korvac, Stark, Dormammu

ENERGY PROJECTION	STRENGTH	DURABILITY	FIGHTING SKILL	INTELLIGENCE	SPEED
1	4	5	4	3	2

POWER RANK

CLOUD 9

Teenager Abby Boylen only wanted to use her mutant powers to fly, but War Machine spotted her in a cloud and forced her to join the Initiative. There, she met fellow student MVP, whose death badly affected her. Norman Osborn tried to use her as an assassin, but she resisted, intentionally missing Night Thrasher when sent to kill him.

Despite her shyness, Cloud 9 has become a leading member of the Initiative. She has fought alongside War Machine and other heroes against such enemies as the Skrulls, Nightmare, Ragnarok, and Hydra.

SKY RIDER
Abby's ability to ride her own personal cloud makes her the perfect hero for espionage and stealth missions.

It is not known what kind of gas Cloud 9 uses to create her clouds.

Abby's ability to conceal herself in a cloud has led villains to try to use her as an assassin.

VITAL STATS
REAL NAME Abigail "Abby" Boylen
OCCUPATION Student
BASE Montana
HEIGHT 5 ft 5 in (1.65 m)
WEIGHT 100 lbs (45.25 kg)
EYES Blue **HAIR** Blonde
POWERS Abby controls a cloud of gas that she can float on and hide inside. She can also use the cloud to surround others and blind or even suffocate them.
ALLIES MVP, Think Tank, Spinner, War Machine (James Rhodes)
FOES KIA, Equinox, Norman Osborn, Skrulls, Ragnarok, Nightmare

POWER RANK	ENERGY PROJECTION	STRENGTH	DURABILITY	FIGHTING SKILL	INTELLIGENCE	SPEED
	4	2	2	4	2	3

COLLECTOR

The Collector is one of the powerful and ancient Elders of the Universe. Born billions of years ago in Cygnus X-1, he is imbued with the Power Primordial, an energy created during the Big Bang. When the Collector believed that the Titan Thanos would destroy the universe, he began collecting specimens of every race to preserve for the future. His attempts to add the Avengers to his collection have all ended in failure.

The Collector once bet Grandmaster that his own team of villains, called the Offenders, could defeat Grandmaster's Defenders.

The Collector's powers of telepathy allow him to communicate with the other Elders.

THE COLLECTION
The Collector once tried to "save" the Avengers from Korvac by adding them to his collection of creatures.

His body is immune to cellular aging and can regenerate from almost any injury.

VITAL STATS
REAL NAME Taneleer Tivan
OCCUPATION Curator
BASE Mobile
HEIGHT 6 ft 2 in (1.87 m)
WEIGHT 450 lbs (204 kg)
EYES White **HAIR** White
POWERS The Collector is immortal and immune to the aging process. He possesses telepathic powers and an ability to alter his size at will by manipulating cosmic energy. He can also use cosmic energy for both attack and defense. His body is impervious to disease and cannot be injured by any conventional means.
ALLIES Grandmaster, Elders of the Universe
FOES Avengers, Thanos

ENERGY PROJECTION	STRENGTH	DURABILITY	FIGHTING SKILL	INTELLIGENCE	SPEED	POWER RANK
4	4	6	2	4	2	

COUNT NEFARIA

Italian nobleman Count Luchino Nefaria was a major member of the Maggia crime family. When he was opposed by the Avengers he had them framed for treason, but they were cleared. After a string of further defeats, Nefaria was given the powers of the Living Laser (energy projection), Power Man (strength), and Whirlwind (speed) by one of Baron Zemo's scientists—but increased a thousand-fold, making him a truly deadly Super Villain.

Count Nefaria's amazing powers are more than enough to hold a full-strength team of Avengers at bay. He has come close to defeating them on several occasions, sometimes with just a single attack.

VITAL STATS

REAL NAME Count Luchino Nefaria

OCCUPATION Professional criminal

BASE Various, including a castle originally located in Italy but moved to the New Jersey Palisades

HEIGHT 6 ft 2 in (1.87 m)

WEIGHT 230 lbs (104.25 kg)

EYES Blue **HAIR** Black

POWERS With his ionic powers, he has superhuman strength, speed, and resistance to injury. He can fly and project laser beams from his eyes. He maintains his strength by draining energy from other beings.

ALLIES Madame Masque, Legion of the Unliving

FOES Avengers, Thunderbolts

Although once fully human, Count Nefaria is now powered by ionic energy.

COUNT VS. CAP
Captain America once stopped a plan by Count Nefaria to use the creatures of the Savage Land to increase his powers.

His ability to fly does not depend on any external paraphernalia.

POWER RANK	ENERGY PROJECTION	STRENGTH	DURABILITY	FIGHTING SKILL	INTELLIGENCE	SPEED
	6	7	6	3	3	5

CRIMSON DYNAMO

The Crimson Dynamo armor was originally created by Russian scientist Anton Vanko to attack Iron Man, who was viewed as an enemy of the Soviet Union. Vanko later changed sides and fled Russia, taking a job with Tony Stark. He died saving Iron Man's life. Since then, many others have taken on the role of Crimson Dynamo. One of the most recent was teenager Gennady Gavrilov, who gained control of a Mark II version of the Crimson Dynamo armor.

The identity of the latest Crimson Dynamo is unknown. He is a member of Russian Super Hero team the Winter Guard. The team has come into conflict with Iron Man and She-Hulk.

The visor on his helmet fires electrical blasts.

ARMORED BATTLE
The original Crimson Dynamo fought Iron Man several times as the Soviet Union tried to prove its superiority over the U.S.A.

Hand blasters fire bolts of electricity that can stop an attacker in his tracks.

VITAL STATS
REAL NAME Anton Vanko
OCCUPATION Scientist
BASE Moscow
HEIGHT 5 ft 8 in (1.72 m)
WEIGHT 165 lbs (75 kg) without armor; 395 lbs (179.25 kg) with armor
EYES Brown **HAIR** Black
POWERS Crimson Dynamo's computerized armored battle suit provides flight, super-strength, and damage resistance. It has a vast range of built-in weapons including missiles, guns, electrical generators, and a fusion caster mounted on the chest.
ALLIES Winter Guard, Iron Man, Black Widow, War Machine
FOES K.G.B., Skrulls

ENERGY PROJECTION	STRENGTH	DURABILITY	FIGHTING SKILL	INTELLIGENCE	SPEED	POWER RANK
3	5	6	2	2	3	

CROSSBONES

Brock Rumlow was always a brutal thug, but when he crossed paths with the Red Skull, he gained a new name—Crossbones. He became the Red Skull's right-hand man and forged a relationship with the Red Skull's evil daughter, Sin. Since then he's proved to be one of the deadliest villains around. While on a mission with the Thunderbolts team of villains, he was mutated and temporarily gained the power to shoot blasts of fire from his masked face.

Crossbones remained at Sin's side when she sought out the eight mystical hammers sent to Earth by the Serpent during the Asgardian deity's attempt to bring fear to the world.

VITAL STATS
REAL NAME Brock Rumlow
OCCUPATION Mercenary
BASE Mobile
HEIGHT 6 ft 4 in (1.93 m)
WEIGHT 290 lbs (131.5 kg)
EYES Brown **HAIR** Black (dyed brown, shaved bald)
POWERS Crossbones is trained in various martial arts and fighting styles. He is also a pilot and an expert with numerous weapons.
ALLIES Red Skull, Sin, Skeleton Crew, Savage Crims (gang)
FOES Captain America, Winter Soldier, Black Widow, Luke Cage, Sharon Carter, Daredevil

Crossbones is an expert marksman with guns, crossbows, and throwing knives.

Crossbones carries a number of deadly weapons and explosives.

BATTLING THE HAND
While in the Thunderbolts, Crossbones fought the Hand. Man-Thing transported Crossbones and his teammates into their lair.

POWER RANK

	ENERGY PROJECTION	STRENGTH	DURABILITY	FIGHTING SKILL	INTELLIGENCE	SPEED
	1	3	3	5	2	2

CRYSTAL

At the end of their troubled marriage, Crystal's husband, Quicksilver, took their daughter, Luna, from their home on Attilan. He also stole the powerful Terrigen Mists that give the Inhumans their power. Crystal's reaction was severe.

Crystal is a princess of the genetically-altered Inhumans with the power to control the elements. As a teenager, she fell in love with the Human Torch (Johnny Storm). She later married the Avenger Quicksilver, although they divorced. Crystal married the Kree Warrior Ronan to cement an alliance between the Inhumans and the Kree. She later decided to remain with Ronan rather than return home.

Crystal sometimes needs to ingest a serum that makes her less vulnerable to city pollution.

VITAL STATS
REAL NAME Corystalia Amaqulin Maximoff
OCCUPATION Princess
BASE Attilan
HEIGHT 5 ft 6 in (1.67 m)
WEIGHT 110 lbs (50 kg)
EYES Green **HAIR** Red
POWERS Crystal's powers are elemental, allowing her to control earth, wind, air, and fire. As an Inhuman, her physical condition is superior to a normal human's; however pollution affects her badly.
ALLIES Inhumans, Fantastic Four, Ronan, Avengers
FOES Shi'ar, Frightful Four, Blastaar

Crystal's abilities allow her to use the air around her as a powerful weapon.

COMPASSIONATE CRYSTAL
After an invasion by the Shi'ar left the Kree capital devastated, Crystal used her powers to help the survivors.

ENERGY PROJECTION	STRENGTH	DURABILITY	FIGHTING SKILL	INTELLIGENCE	SPEED	POWER RANK
4	2	2	3	2	2	

DAREDEVIL

By day he is Matt Murdock, ace attorney. By night he is Daredevil, protecting the innocent. While Matt is blind, his other senses have reached superhuman levels and combine with a radar sense and martial arts training to make him more than a match for any criminal. To those he helps, he's a guardian angel. To the bad guys, he is the Man Without Fear!

Matt first met Elektra at college. She was the love of his life, but after the death of her father she became a cold-blooded assassin and the couple parted. Elektra returned to help Daredevil when ninja assassins known as the Hand tried to kill him.

VITAL STATS
REAL NAME Matthew Michael Murdock
OCCUPATION Attorney
BASE Currently San Francisco
HEIGHT 5 ft 11 in (1.80 m)
WEIGHT 185 lbs (84 kg)
EYES Blue **HAIR** Red/brown
POWERS Daredevil is totally blind, but his other senses have been superhumanly heightened. He possesses a radar sense that allows him to detect objects around him and is highly trained in various martial arts including kung fu, boxing, karate, and ninjitsu. He carries a club that can be used as an offensive and defensive weapon.
ALLIES Elektra, Stick, Black Widow, Echo
FOES Kingpin, Bullseye, the Hand

The famous "DD" logo inspires terror in the underworld.

The devil's horns on Daredevil's helmet have earned him the nickname "Ol' Hornhead."

ACE OF CLUBS
Daredevil's club can be used as a projectile to defeat opponents as well as to defend him from attack.

Daredevil's senses are so acute he can read newsprint just by touching it.

POWER RANK	ENERGY PROJECTION	STRENGTH	DURABILITY	FIGHTING SKILL	INTELLIGENCE	SPEED
	4	3	2	5	3	2

DEATHLOK

The latest Deathlok is Henry Hayes, a combat medic who lost a leg while on duty in Kandahar. Biotek replaced his missing limb—but also turned him into a cyborg assassin. Hayes has no knowledge of his missions—or the people he has assassinated. When Biotek issue him with their codeword, he becomes their deadly assassin, killing whomever they order him to. His connection to previous incarnations of Deathlok remains unrevealed.

Deathlok has been used as a soldier and as an assassin. S.H.I.E.L.D. agent Seth Horne told Hayes that he was Deathlok. Deathlok was then ordered by his controllers to terminate Horne, to keep the Deathlok program secret.

Cybernetic eye glows red when Deathlok is operational.

Deathlok is expert with various types of state-of-the-art weaponry.

VITAL STATS

REAL NAME Henry Hayes
OCCUPATION Former combat medic now working with Doctors Without Borders, mercenary super-soldier
BASE Philadelphia, PA
HEIGHT 6 ft 2 in (1.87 m)
WEIGHT 325 lbs (147.5 kg)
EYES Brown, red when activated
HAIR Black
POWERS Superhuman strength, speed, and durability. Computer-enhanced senses and reflexes. Computer-enhanced targeting. Enhanced sight and hearing. Proficiency with melee weapons, firearms, and heavy ordnance.
ALLIES/FOES Not applicable

AN AVENGERS FRIEND
An earlier incarnation of Deathlok fought alongside Captain America and the Avengers.

ENERGY PROJECTION	STRENGTH	DURABILITY	FIGHTING SKILL	INTELLIGENCE	SPEED	POWER RANK
1	6	3	4	3	3	

DEMOLITION MAN

Dennis Dunphy was a professional wrestler who had his powers increased by a villain called the Power Broker. He became so strong that he was even capable of taking on the Thing! Dennis adopted an outfit based on that of his hero, Daredevil. Now known as Demolition Man, he fought alongside Captain America and the Avengers several times. He was killed while in the role of the Scourge.

Dunphy once began to suffer from delusions and took to living in the sewers. Reporter Ben Urich persuaded him to get help.

VITAL STATS
REAL NAME Dennis Dunphy
OCCUPATION Adventurer
BASE New York City
HEIGHT 6 ft 3 in (1.90 m)
WEIGHT 396 lbs (179.50 kg)
EYES Blue **HAIR** Red
POWERS Demolition Man possessed superhuman strength and endurance. He was also a wrestler and fought in the Unlimited Class Wrestling Federation. His strength was sometimes affected by a heart condition.
ALLIES Captain America, Thing
FOES Flag Smasher, Morgan Le Fay, Mordred

His muscular, wrestler's body was enhanced still further by the Power Broker.

His costume was based on Daredevil's first outfit combined with Wolverine's headpiece.

WEAK HEART
Dunphy fought alongside the Avengers against Morgan Le Fay before a weak heart forced him to step back from life as a Super Hero.

POWER RANK

ENERGY PROJECTION	STRENGTH	DURABILITY	FIGHTING SKILL	INTELLIGENCE	SPEED
1	4	3	5	1	2

DIAMONDBACK

Athlete Rachel Leighton was trained to fight by the Taskmaster and joined the criminal Serpent Society as Diamondback. But while on a mission against Captain America, she became smitten by the hero and left the Society. She fought alongside Captain America for a while, joining his Secret Avengers team during the Super Hero Civil War. Diamondback later became an agent of S.H.I.E.LD.

Diamondback formed B.A.D. Girls Inc. with Asp and Black Mamba partly to protect themselves after they left the Serpent Society. They also took on mercenary jobs—one of which brought them into conflict with Deadpool.

Her throwing spikes may contain anything from snake venom to sleep-inducing drugs.

VITAL STATS
REAL NAME Rachel Leighton
OCCUPATION S.H.I.E.L.D. agent
BASE Camp Hammond
HEIGHT 5 ft 11 in (1.80 m)
WEIGHT 142 lbs (64.50 kg)
EYES Green **HAIR** Magenta
POWERS: She is an expert gymnast, and uses diamond-shaped throwing spikes that are sometimes filled with explosives or other deadly substances.
ALLIES Captain America, the Constrictor, Asp, Black Mamba
FOES The Serpent Society

REVENGE OF THE SERPENTS
The Serpent Society sought revenge on Diamondback after she betrayed them because of her feelings for Captain America.

ENERGY PROJECTION	STRENGTH	DURABILITY	FIGHTING SKILL	INTELLIGENCE	SPEED	POWER RANK
1	3	3	4	2	2	

DINAH SOAR

Dinah Soar's origins are a mystery but it is possible she was born in the Savage Land. She was an expert in flight and proved to be a valued member of the Great Lakes Avengers. Mr. Immortal was the only team member who could hear Dinah Soar's hypersonic voice, and the two were romantically involved. Dinah fought with the team against Deadpool, the Thunderbolts, and Graviton but was tragically killed during a fight with the rogue Inhuman, Maelstrom.

Dinah Soar was a fast and acrobatic flyer, swooping into attacks with ease.

VITAL STATS
REAL NAME Unknown
OCCUPATION Adventurer
BASE Great Lakes
HEIGHT Unrevealed
WEIGHT Unrevealed
EYES Black **HAIR** None
POWERS: Dinah Soar could fly. She also had a hypersonic voice that only Mr. Immortal could hear.
ALLIES Mr. Immortal, Doorway, Big Bertha
FOES Graviton, Maelstrom

TEAM PLAYER
For a time, Dinah Soar was a valued member of the Great Lakes Avengers.

Dinah's claws were extremely sharp and she had razor-tipped wings.

POWER RANK	ENERGY PROJECTION	STRENGTH	DURABILITY	FIGHTING SKILL	INTELLIGENCE	SPEED
	4	2	2	3	2	3

DOCTOR DRUID

Doctor Druid was a master of the occult who was trained by the Ancient One, a famous sorcerer. He used his magical powers to help others, and joined the Avengers after freeing their mansion from the control of the Masters of Evil. However, Doctor Druid was also easily manipulated. Terminatrix once used him to attack his fellow Avengers, and he eventually fell under the influence of the demon Slorioth before being killed by Daimon Hellstrom, the Son of Satan.

Doctor Druid and a disguised Terminatrix plotted against the Avengers.

Doctor Druid's robes reflected his interest in ancient forms of sorcery.

VITAL STATS

REAL NAME Doctor Anthony Ludgate Druid
OCCUPATION Psychiatrist, master of the occult
BASE Mobile
HEIGHT 6 ft 5 in (1.95 m)
WEIGHT 310 lbs (140.5 kg)
EYES Green **HAIR** Black
POWERS He was a master of the mystic arts, was telepathic, could levitate himself or other objects, and control his own heartbeat, breathing, and bleeding.
ALLIES Doctor Strange, Ancient One, Avengers
FOES Nekra, Masters of Evil, Terminatrix

TRAITOR IN THE RANKS
Doctor Druid turned on his teammates and tried to kill them while under the influence of the time-traveling Terminatrix.

ENERGY PROJECTION	STRENGTH	DURABILITY	FIGHTING SKILL	INTELLIGENCE	SPEED	POWER RANK
4	2	2	3	3	2	

DOCTOR STRANGE

Doctor Stephen Strange was once a brilliant surgeon but lost his ability to perform surgery after a car accident. He sought out the Ancient One hoping to find a way of healing himself, but instead succeeded him as Earth's Sorcerer Supreme. Since then he has been Earth's mystical champion and battled villains such as the demon Dormammu and Baron Mordo, both on his own and as part of the Defenders and the Avengers Super Hero teams.

As Sorcerer Supreme, Strange employed a variety of magical objects to increase his powers. These included a powerful amulet called the Eye of Agamotto, a Cloak of Levitation, and a large library of mystic books.

AVENGER
Doctor Strange remained an Avenger even when he briefly lost his position as Sorcerer Supreme.

VITAL STATS

REAL NAME Doctor Stephen Vincent Strange
OCCUPATION Former surgeon, ex-Sorcerer Supreme of Earth
BASE Greenwich Village, Manhattan
HEIGHT 6 ft 2 in (1.87 m)
WEIGHT 180 lbs (81.75 kg)
EYES Gray **HAIR** Black, (gray at temples)
POWERS One of the most powerful sorcerers in existence, Strange can perform astral projection, teleport, and cast numerous spells. He is also a skilled martial artist and doctor.
ALLIES Clea, Hulk, Sub-Mariner, Avengers, Defenders
FOES Baron Mordo, Dormammu, Nightmare

A mystical amulet, the Eye of Agamotto, is given to the Sorcerer Supreme in order to expand his powers.

The Cloak of Levitation allows him to fly without using up stores of magical energy.

POWER RANK	ENERGY PROJECTION	STRENGTH	DURABILITY	FIGHTING SKILL	INTELLIGENCE	SPEED
	6	2	3	3	4	7

DOCTOR VOODOO

When Jericho Drumm's twin brother, Daniel, was killed by an evil houngan (voodoo priest) named Damballah, Jericho learned voodoo and defeated the houngan. He was later selected by Doctor Strange's amulet, the Eye of Agamotto, as the new Sorcerer Supreme and renamed Doctor Voodoo. He seemingly died saving the world from the entity known as Agamotto.

In his new role as Sorcerer Supreme, Doctor Voodoo joined forces with Doctor Doom to take on Nightmare.

VITAL STATS

REAL NAME Jericho Drumm
OCCUPATION Sorcerer Supreme, houngan (voodoo priest)
BASE Mobile
HEIGHT 6 ft (1.82 m)
WEIGHT 220 lbs (99.75 kg)
EYES Brown
HAIR Brown/white
POWERS As the Sorcerer Supreme, Drumm had possession of the Cloak of Levitation and the Eye of Agamotto. His strength is doubled when he is possessed by his brother's spirit and he can send this spirit to possess others.
ALLIES Black Panther, Doctor Strange, Heroes for Hire, Avengers
FOES Baron Samedi, Nightmare, Dormammu

The Cloak of Levitation and the Eye of Agamotto increased his powers.

He carried the Staff of Legba, which bears two heads that speak a mystic language.

HELLSTROM
Doctor Voodoo faced countless supernatural dangers, including Daimon Hellstrom, the Son of Satan.

ENERGY PROJECTION	STRENGTH	DURABILITY	FIGHTING SKILL	INTELLIGENCE	SPEED	POWER RANK
6	4	3	3	3	3	

DOORMAN

DeMarr Davis was gifted with the mutant power of teleportation. As Doorman he was a founding member of the Great Lakes Avengers, but he died fighting the Inhuman, Maelstrom. The cosmically powered being known as Oblivion chose Doorman as the new Angel of Death, and he now escorts spirits to the afterlife. He has also returned to join his friends in the renamed Great Lakes Champions.

Doorman has access to the Darkforce Dimension but can only use it to benefit others by teleporting them into the next room. He does this by turning his whole body into a transdimensional gateway people can pass through.

VITAL STATS

REAL NAME DeMarr Davis
OCCUPATION Adventurer, Angel of Death
BASE Unrevealed
HEIGHT 5 ft 10 in (1.77 m)
WEIGHT 180 lbs (81.50 kg)
EYES Brown
HAIR Black
POWERS He can open gateways into the Darkforce Dimension, a strange realm beyond normal reality.
ALLIES Mr. Immortal, Dinah Soar, Big Bertha, Flatman, Squirrel Girl
FOES Maelstrom, Deadpool

He can alter his body so objects pass straight through him.

LIFE AFTER DEATH
Death was not the end for Doorman. Oblivion remade him as the Angel of Death.

Doorman's body is a gateway to the Darkforce Dimension.

POWER RANK	ENERGY PROJECTION	STRENGTH	DURABILITY	FIGHTING SKILL	INTELLIGENCE	SPEED
	3	2	7	3	7	7

DORMAMMU

Dormammu, ruler of the Dark Dimension, has sought to take over Earth countless times. He once joined Loki in an attempt to obtain the magical object known as the Evil Eye, and the evil pair engineered a conflict between the Avengers and the Defenders. Dormammu also gave the superpowered criminal the Hood his terrifying power. Dormammu is trapped in his own realm, but the day will surely come when he tries to invade Earth once again.

Dormammu once tried to kill a weakened Doctor Strange, but Strange's teammates in the Avengers stopped him.

To fend off attackers, he can harness the power of the Dark Dimension.

Dormammu is made of pure mystical energy, and can take any form he chooses.

VITAL STATS

REAL NAME Dormammu
OCCUPATION
Ruler of the Dark Dimension
BASE Dark Dimension
HEIGHT Varies depending on form: 6 ft 1 in (1.85 m) in human form
WEIGHT Variable
EYES Yellow (green in human form)
HAIR None (black (in human form)
POWERS One of the most powerful mystical creatures in the universe and a master of sorcery, Dormammu can teleport between dimensions, travel through time, perform telepathy, and alter his size or form at will.
ALLIES Umar, the Mindless Ones
FOES Doctor Voodoo, Doctor Strange, Avengers, Clea

MAGICAL ENEMIES
Dormammu has had numerous battles with Earth's Sorcerer Supreme and has a special hatred of Doctor Strange.

ENERGY PROJECTION	STRENGTH	DURABILITY	FIGHTING SKILL	INTELLIGENCE	SPEED	POWER RANK
7	7	7	4	6	7	

DRAX THE DESTROYER

Drax was originally a real-estate agent named Arthur Douglas. He was driving across the desert with his wife and daughter when they were attacked by the mad Titan Thanos, who wanted to keep his arrival on Earth secret. Arthur's wife was killed, but the Titan god Kronus saved Arthur's consciousness and placed it in a powerful, artificial body. Drax has since cut a deadly path across the galaxy hunting for Thanos. Arthur's daughter Heather also survived Thanos' attack and became Moondragon.

Drax has joined several incarnations of the Guardians of the Galaxy and has proved to be one of the team's most powerful members.

VITAL STATS
REAL NAME Arthur Sampson Douglas
OCCUPATION Adventurer
BASE Mobile
HEIGHT 6 ft 4 in (1.93 m)
WEIGHT 680 lbs (308.5 kg)
EYES Red **HAIR** None
POWERS Drax possesses superhuman strength, endurance, and durability and is an expert fighter, favoring knives. He can survive indefinitely without food or water. He also has the ability to psychically track Thanos.
ALLIES Guardians of the Galaxy, Nova, Venom (Flash Thompson)
FOES Thanos, Annihilus

Drax's body is extremely tough and he can regenerate from near-fatal wounds.

In his current form, Drax can no longer fly or fire cosmic blasts.

Mortal Enemies
Drax and Thanos have fought several times. Drax has even killed Thanos—only for the Titan to be reborn.

POWER RANK	ENERGY PROJECTION	STRENGTH	DURABILITY	FIGHTING SKILL	INTELLIGENCE	SPEED
	1	5	7	4	2	2

DUM DUM DUGAN

Ex-circus strongman Timothy "Dum Dum" Dugan (his nickname comes from a type of bullet) fought alongside Nick Fury Sr. in World War II. He then became a S.H.I.E.L.D. agent, and his aging process was slowed using technology. During the Super Hero Civil War Dugan was ordered to hunt Captain America—something he later regretted. It was later revealed that Dugan had died in the past, and that Fury had replaced him with a Life Model Decoy.

Dum Dum Dugan has been an ally of Wolverine for decades. He helped his old pal take revenge on the Hand when the ninja organization tried to brainwash him.

FRIEND OF FURY
Dugan first fought alongside Nick Fury as part of the Howling Commandos in World War II.

This gun holster on top of his costume provides easy access to weapons in case of attack.

Dugan is a former strongman, and is known for his powerful physique.

VITAL STATS
REAL NAME Timothy Aloysius Cadwallader "Dum Dum" Dugan
OCCUPATION Ex-S.H.I.E.L.D. agent, now part of Nick Fury's Secret Warriors team
BASE New York City
HEIGHT 6 ft 2 in (1.87 m)
WEIGHT 260 lbs (118 kg)
EYES Blue
HAIR Red
POWERS Dugan is an expert wrestler, soldier, boxer, and spy.
ALLIES Nick Fury, Wolverine
FOES Hydra, the Hand

ENERGY PROJECTION	STRENGTH	DURABILITY	FIGHTING SKILL	INTELLIGENCE	SPEED	POWER RANK
1	2	2	4	2	2	

ECHO

When Willie "Crazy Horse" Lincoln was killed by Wilson Fisk the Kingpin of Crime, his dying wish was for Fisk to take care of his deaf daughter, Maya. Kingpin raised her as his own child, and told her that Daredevil had killed her father. Maya swore to avenge his death. She trained in martial arts, took the name Echo, and tried to kill Daredevil. While helping Moon Knight, she was killed in action by Count Nefaria.

Echo took on the role of Ronin, joining the Avengers. Together they fought the assassins known as the Hand.

VITAL STATS

REAL NAME Maya Lopez
OCCUPATION Adventurer, performance artist
BASE Japan
HEIGHT 5 ft 9 in (1.75 m)
WEIGHT 125 lbs (56.75 kg)
EYES Brown
HAIR Black
POWERS When she was a child, it was thought that Maya had learning difficulties. This was proved wrong; however she was deaf. Maya could copy any action she saw, such as fighting or acrobatics. She was also a martial artist and pianist.
ALLIES Daredevil, Wolverine
FOES Kingpin, Silver Samurai, the Hand

A handprint painted on her face was in memory of the bloodied handprint left by her dying father.

After watching another person, Echo could mimic their physical abilities exactly.

BOY TROUBLE
Maya fell in love with Matt Murdock, not realizing that his alter ego was the man she believed had killed her father—Daredevil!

POWER RANK

ENERGY PROJECTION	STRENGTH	DURABILITY	FIGHTING SKILL	INTELLIGENCE	SPEED
1	2	2	6	4	2

EGGHEAD

Egghead saw Hank Pym as his main rival and tried to kill him many times. The two first clashed when Pym was in his Ant-Man persona.

The original Egghead was a mad scientist named Elihas Starr. He worked for the government but was caught smuggling blueprints and sent to jail. After being freed from jail, Egghead resumed his scientific career, and went on to develop a fierce rivalry with Hank Pym who was just starting out as Ant-Man. The Super Villain and Super Hero clashed on many occasions, but Egghead was not able to defeat Pym. Egghead even led one version of the Masters of Evil against the Avengers.

Elihas was dubbed "Egghead" by the press because of his strangely shaped head.

VITAL STATS
REAL NAME Elihas Starr
OCCUPATION Criminal, scientist
BASE New York City
HEIGHT 5 ft 7 in (1.70 m)
WEIGHT 320 lbs (145 kg)
EYES Blue **HAIR** None
POWERS Starr uses his scientific knowledge to create powerful robots, mind controlling limbs, and other strange machines, including one that allows him to talk to ants.
ALLIES Mad Thinker, Puppet Master, the Rhino
FOES Ant-Man (original), Avengers, Defenders

THE NEW EGGHEAD
A new villain calling himself Egghead appeared as part of the Young Masters. His origins are still unknown but he appears to have the power to manipulate minds, steal memories, plant false ones, and cause comas.

ENERGY PROJECTION	STRENGTH	DURABILITY	FIGHTING SKILL	INTELLIGENCE	SPEED	POWER RANK
3	2	3	2	6	3	

ELECTRO

Electric company employee Max Dillon gained his electrical-based powers when lightning struck him while he was fixing some electrical power lines. Dillon created a criminal alter ego called Electro, and wearing a colorful costume began a crime spree. He attracted the attention of Spider-Man almost immediately. Soon Electro had become one of Spidey's main adversaries and the two would face each other many times.

Electro was once hired to break the terrorist Sauron out of the Raft, a high-security prison for Super Villains. He started the breakout by short-circuiting the prison's electrical systems. A new team of Avengers was formed to track down the escaped criminals, as well as Electro himself.

VITAL STATS

REAL NAME Maxwell Dillon
OCCUPATION Former power company employee, criminal
BASE New York City
HEIGHT 5 ft 11 in (1.80 m)
WEIGHT 165 lbs (74.75 kg)
EYES Blue
HAIR Red/brown
POWERS Electro can generate large amounts of electricity, drain it from the nearby environment, and attack enemies with deadly electrical shocks.
ALLIES Sinister Six, Frightful Four, Emissaries of Evil
FOES Spider-Man, Avengers, Kaine

When fully charged, Electro is extremely vulnerable to anything that can "short circuit" his abilities, such as water.

His fingertips fire lightning bolts that have a range of up to 100 ft (30.5 m).

FIRST FOE
Over the years Electro's hatred for Spider-Man has grown, due to the many defeats he has suffered at the web-slinger's hands.

POWER RANK

ENERGY PROJECTION	STRENGTH	DURABILITY	FIGHTING SKILL	INTELLIGENCE	SPEED
5	2	3	2	2	2

ELEKTRA

Elektra Natchios is the ex-girlfriend of Matt Murdock (Daredevil). When Elektra's father was killed she left Matt and joined the Hand, a group of deadly assassins. She eventually became their leader, but was killed by Maya Lopez after a conflict with the New Avengers. However, the Elektra who died was found to be a Skrull and the real Elektra was freed from Skrull captivity during the Skrull Invasion. Since then, Elektra has returned to her life as an assassin.

While working for the crime lord Kingpin, Elektra was faced with the possibility of having to kill Daredevil, her former boyfriend.

THUNDERBOLTS
Elektra joined the Thunderbolts. Her teammates included the Red Hulk, Punisher, Venom and Deadpool.

Elektra is an accomplished athlete and gymnast, with great strength, speed, agility, reflexes, and endurance.

Elektra's twin sai are a pair of delicate but deadly daggers with three prongs.

VITAL STATS
REAL NAME Elektra Natchios
OCCUPATION Mercenary, assassin
BASE Mobile
HEIGHT 5 ft 9 in (1.75 m)
WEIGHT 130 lbs (59 kg)
EYES Blue/black
HAIR Black
POWERS Elektra possesses exceptional martial arts skills, outstanding gymnastic and athletic abilities, some limited telepathic skills, and control of her own nervous system.
ALLIES Daredevil, Wolverine, Nick Fury Sr.
FOES The Hand, Bullseye, Kingpin

ENERGY PROJECTION	STRENGTH	DURABILITY	FIGHTING SKILL	INTELLIGENCE	SPEED
1	2	3	6	3	2

POWER RANK

ENCHANTRESS

Amora the Enchantress is a sorceress from Asgard, home of the Norse gods. Few men are able to resist her beauty, and those who can are soon fixed by a spell. She enchanted the Black Knight into fighting against the Defenders, only to turn him to stone with a kiss afterward. After banishment from Asgard, the Enchantress joined a new incarnation of the villainous Sisterhood of Mutants.

The Enchantress was part of Baron Zemo's original Masters of Evil group, and was thus one of the first foes the Avengers faced.

VITAL STATS

REAL NAME Amora
OCCUPATION Sorceress
BASE Asgard
HEIGHT 6 ft 3 in (1.90 m)
WEIGHT 450 lbs (204 kg)
EYES Green **HAIR** Blonde
POWERS Amora's kiss can enslave any man. She has exceptional magical knowledge, and she possesses the extra strength, lifespan, and power of a goddess.
ALLIES Loki, the Executioner, Baron Zemo
FOES Thor, the Black Knight, Avengers

Amora appears even more beautiful than usual to men she has enslaved.

She is able to harness magical energy and use it as a physical or mystical weapon.

SPELL CASTER
Using a spell, the Enchantress can spy on her enemy's actions from her home in Asgard.

POWER RANK	ENERGY PROJECTION	STRENGTH	DURABILITY	FIGHTING SKILL	INTELLIGENCE	SPEED
	6	4	6	2	4	2

EX NIHILO

Ex Nihilo is a powerful avatar of creation known as a Gardener, seeding worlds to improve them. While bringing life to Mars, he met the Avengers and when his work threatened Earth, came into conflict with them. He later joined the Avengers on the urging of Captain Universe. Ex Nihilo used his exceptional powers to help the Avengers fight the Builders and to save the world from a potentially devastating attack from a parallel reality.

Ex Nihilo first met the Avengers as he brought life to Mars. He quickly captured the team but later became a key member.

Ex Nihilo means "out of nothing" in Latin—and so is an especially suitable name for this mysterious being.

The purpose of Ex Nihilo's horns is unknown.

VITAL STATS
REAL NAME Ex Nihilo
OCCUPATION Gardener, avatar of creation
BASE Mobile
HEIGHT Unrevealed
WEIGHT Unrevealed
EYES Green **HAIR** None
POWERS The extent of Ex Nihilo's powers is unknown. He can grow plants, create new life forms, and change planets' atmospheres. He can also fire blasts of energy.
ALLIES Abyss, Captain Universe
FOES Thanos, Gardeners

A GARDENERS' FOE
Ex Nihilo was shocked to learn other Gardeners had started to destroy worlds rather than improve them.

ENERGY PROJECTION	STRENGTH	DURABILITY	FIGHTING SKILL	INTELLIGENCE	SPEED	POWER RANK
4	4	3	2	6	2	

EXECUTIONER

Skurge the Executioner was an Asgardian warrior often used by the Norse goddess Enchantress in her evil plans. He fought the Avengers and Thor many times, but when the Enchantress left him, Skurge changed sides. He joined Thor on a mission to rescue some trapped mortals from Hel, the Asgardian realm of the dead. The Executioner died a hero, holding back the forces of Hel and giving his allies time to escape.

For many years, Skurge was used by the Enchantress to give her muscular back-up in her many fights against Thor and the Avengers.

HONORABLE DEATH
Skurge died saving Thor's life and helping trapped soldiers escape from Hel. His name is spoken with honor in Asgard because of his heroic sacrifice.

As well as his magical ax, Skurge could use powerful energy blasts in battle.

Skurge's huge build was inherited from his father, a Frost Giant.

VITAL STATS
REAL NAME Skurge
OCCUPATION Giant-killer
BASE Asgard
HEIGHT 7 ft 2 in (2.18 m)
WEIGHT 1,100 lbs (499 kg)
EYES Blue **HAIR** Black
POWERS He had superhuman strength and stamina, exceptional fighting skills, a magical ax that allowed time travel, and could fire blasts of energy. He also possessed an unbreakable helmet.
ALLIES The Enchantress, Thor
FOES The Avengers, Hel

POWER RANK	ENERGY PROJECTION	STRENGTH	DURABILITY	FIGHTING SKILL	INTELLIGENCE	SPEED
	5	7	6	6	4	4

FALCON

Since first teaming up together, Falcon and Captain America were close allies. Sam eventually took on the role of Captain America.

Sam Wilson, the Falcon, was a criminal until he met evil mastermind the Red Skull, who gave Sam the ability to communicate telepathically with his pet falcon, Redwing. The Skull planned to have Sam befriend his archenemy Captain America and later betray Cap, but the scheme failed. Sam's heroic nature overcame the Skull's programming and he became a crime fighter instead. Over the years, Sam has developed the ability to communicate with all birds, not just Redwing.

FLYING HIGH TECH
Advanced technology from the Black Panther gave the Falcon the ability to fly.

Falcon is an accomplished bird trainer and a highly trained gymnast.

VITAL STATS
REAL NAME Sam "Snap" Wilson
OCCUPATION Super Hero, urban planner
BASE Harlem, New York City
HEIGHT 6 ft 2 in (1.87 m)
WEIGHT 240 lbs (108.75 kg)
EYES Brown **HAIR** Black
POWERS He has a telepathic link with Redwing, his trained falcon. Jet-powered wings enable him to fly, and he has exceptional fighting skills.
ALLIES Captain America, Sharon Carter, Black Widow, Black Panther
FOES Red Skull

ENERGY PROJECTION	STRENGTH	DURABILITY	FIGHTING SKILL	INTELLIGENCE	SPEED	POWER RANK
1	2	2	4	2	3	

FINESSE

Jeanne Foucault can master any skill just by watching. A teenage prodigy, she was training for the Olympics when she was kidnapped by U.S. security chief Norman Osborn, who hoped to use her powers for his own evil purposes. After Osborn's fall from power, the Avengers took over Jeanne's education, hoping to guide her into becoming a hero. She is an expert in a variety of fighting styles but appears cold and aloof. Human emotions are the one thing she can't comprehend.

Finesse believes Taskmaster might be her father. The two met and have similar powers but Taskmaster's memory lapses prevent him from knowing for sure.

VITAL STATS
REAL NAME Jeanne Foucault
OCCUPATION Students
BASE Avengers Academy
HEIGHT 5 ft 4 in (1.63 m)
WEIGHT 110 lbs (50 kg)
EYES Blue **HAIR** Black
POWERS Finesse is a polymath, an expert in numerous things including many fighting arts. She acquires skills with amazing speed—she learned martial arts just by watching movies.
ALLIES Hazmat, Reptil, Mettle, Striker, Veil, Taskmaster, Avengers
FOES Norman Osborn, Korvac, Psycho-Man

Finesse is unable to connect with people on a personal level.

EVIL SECRETS
Hoping to improve her fighting skills, Finesse tried to persuade Quicksilver to tell her the secrets of his training while he was with the Brotherhood of Evil Mutants.

Finesse favors billy clubs when fighting.

POWER RANK

ENERGY PROJECTION	STRENGTH	DURABILITY	FIGHTING SKILL	INTELLIGENCE	SPEED
1	2	2	5	4	2

FIREBIRD

Bonita Juarez gained control over fire when a meteor crashed to Earth and nearly hit her. As Firebird, she used her powers to help protect the American Southwest, joining forces with the West Coast Avengers to fight Master Pandemonium. She later found out that the meteor was a failed experiment by a race of alien scholars. Firebird fought alongside Captain America and the Secret Avengers during the Super Hero Civil War and joined the Texas Rangers.

Firebird recently joined Gravity, Venom, Moduoo, Waop, and Spider-Man fighting on a strange, alien world as part of an intergalactic game. Spider-Man was revealed to be a Space-Phantom, and was killed by Venom shortly after their arrival.

Firebird uses her mind to control any nearby heat or flame.

TWISTED REALITY
The Avengers were once taken to a reality altered by Morgan le Fay, with Firebird fighting as one of her guards!

She is immune to extreme heat and fire and can create powerful winds by manipulating air temperatures.

VITAL STATS
REAL NAME Bonita Juarez
OCCUPATION Social worker
BASE New Mexico
HEIGHT 5 ft 5 in (1.65 m)
WEIGHT 125 lbs (56.75 kg)
EYES Brown **HAIR** Black
POWERS She can generate a field of fire around her that looks like a bird and also enables her to fly.
ALLIES Avengers, Texas Rangers
FOES Morgan Le Fay, Dominex, Bloodwraith

ENERGY PROJECTION	STRENGTH	DURABILITY	FIGHTING SKILL	INTELLIGENCE	SPEED	POWER RANK
5	2	7	3	3	5	

FLATMAN

Doctor Val Ventura is an astrophysicist and second in command of the Great Lakes Avengers. He can stretch his body into various shapes but can never be anything other than two-dimensional, hence his Super Hero name—Flatman. Val's teammates once thought he had died fighting Maelstrom but it turned out that Val had just turned sideways due to the embarrassment of losing his clothes in the fight.

Flatman's powers are similar to those of Mr. Fantastic, but he is not as elastic as the leader of the Fantastic Four. He is apparently permanently stuck in his two-dimensional state.

VITAL STATS
REAL NAME Val Ventura
OCCUPATION Astrophysicist
BASE The Great Lakes, U.S.A.
HEIGHT 5 ft 2 in (1.57 m), but varies when he stretches
WEIGHT 101 lbs (45.75 kg)
EYES Blue **HAIR** Light brown
POWERS Flatman possesses a thin, two-dimensional body that can stretch and be molded into a variety of shapes.
ALLIES Mr. Immortal, Doorman, Big Bertha, Squirrel Girl
FOES Maelstrom, Deadpool

A two-dimensional body allows Flatman to go unnoticed when he turns sideways.

NAME CHANGES
The Great Lakes Avengers changed their name a number of times, choosing the Great Lakes Champions and the Great Lakes X-Men before reverting to their original name.

POWER RANK

	ENERGY PROJECTION	STRENGTH	DURABILITY	FIGHTING SKILL	INTELLIGENCE	SPEED
	1	3	5	5	3	2

GAMORA

When Gamora's race was wiped out, she was adopted by the mad Titan Thanos. He trained her to be an assassin—hoping to use her to kill his rival, Magus (an evil, future version of Adam Warlock). When Gamora learned the true nature and motives of her "father" she turned against Thanos and helped Adam Warlock defeat him. Since then, she has used her assassin's skills to help others, sometimes as part of the Guardians of the Galaxy.

Gamora's fighting skills are the result of years of training. Her durability and strength have been upgraded on various occasions, making her one of the most feared opponents in the universe.

Gamora is proficient in the use of most known weapons.

Thanos enhanced her natural speed, agility, and durability.

VITAL STATS

REAL NAME Gamora
OCCUPATION Adventurer, former assassin
BASE Mobile
HEIGHT 6 ft (1.83 m)
WEIGHT 170 lbs (77 kg)
EYES Yellow **HAIR** Black
POWERS Gamora's natural abilities have been enhanced. Her skeleton is a near-indestructible alloy, allowing her to survive falls that would kill others. A superb athlete and fighter, she has a favorite sword named Godslayer.
ALLIES Guardians of the Galaxy, Angela, Adam Warlock, Pip, Nova
FOES Thanos, Annihilus and the Phalanx, Magus

POWER COUPLE
Nova (Richard Rider) persuaded Gamora to join the Guardians of the Galaxy. The pair also had a stormy relationship.

ENERGY PROJECTION	STRENGTH	DURABILITY	FIGHTING SKILL	INTELLIGENCE	SPEED	POWER RANK
1	3	3	6	3	4	

GAUNTLET

Soldier Joseph Green was sent to the Sudanese desert to investigate alien weaponry that had crashed to Earth. When Hydra attacked, he was forced to use a strange, alien gauntlet that he had found in the wreckage in defense. Green survived, but the weapon bonded to his arm. He went on to become chief instructor of the Initiative at Camp Hammond but fled when Norman Osborn tried to take the gauntlet. He later joined the Avengers: Resistance, who opposed Osborn's regime.

Gauntlet was forced into a one-on-one battle with Thor's clone, Ragnarok, when it was rebuilt by Skrull technology.

VITAL STATS

REAL NAME Joseph Green
OCCUPATION Ex-soldier, Super Hero trainer
BASE Camp Hammond, Stamford, Connecticut
HEIGHT 5 ft 11 in (1.80 m)
WEIGHT 197 lbs (89.25 kg)
EYES Brown **HAIR** Black
POWERS The alien gauntlet on his right arm enables him to project blasts of energy.
ALLIES Avengers: Resistance
FOES KIA, Norman Osborn

The gauntlet is made from unknown alien material, and is very strong and durable.

Joseph later returned to the army, serving in Afghanistan.

BLASTING POWER
Green's alien gauntlet can fire energy blasts but the true extent of its power has yet to be discovered.

POWER RANK

ENERGY PROJECTION	STRENGTH	DURABILITY	FIGHTING SKILL	INTELLIGENCE	SPEED
4	3	2	4	4	2

GENIS-VELL

Genis-Vell used the names Legacy, Captain Marvel, Pulsar, and Photon during his Super Hero career. During one of the Avengers' many wars with Kang the Conqueror, Rick Jones found himself cosmically connected to Genis-Vell. They aided the Avengers in their fight, but in time Genis-Vell's cosmic powers drove him insane. When his madness threatened the universe, he was apparently killed by Baron Zemo.

Genis-Vell never met his father, Captain Marvel, but he inherited some of his powers.

VITAL STATS
REAL NAME Genis-Vell
OCCUPATION Adventurer
BASE Mobile
HEIGHT 6 ft 2 in (1.87 m)
WEIGHT 210 lbs (95.25 kg)
EYES Blue **HAIR** Blond in human form; white in cosmic form
POWERS Genis-Vell's powers were energy based, like his father's. Nega-bands gave him superhuman strength, speed, and flight. He could also fire energy blasts. His cosmic awareness could sense danger throughout the galaxy.
ALLIES Rick Jones, Moondragon, Avengers
FOES The Time-Keepers, Kang the Conqueror, Baron Zemo

Nega-bands fused energy from the Negative Zone and psionic power to strengthen the wearer.

A translation device implanted under his skin enabled him to understand any language.

KREE COSTUME
When Genis-Vell became unstable, he took to wearing a Kree costume.

ENERGY PROJECTION	STRENGTH	DURABILITY	FIGHTING SKILL	INTELLIGENCE	SPEED	POWER RANK
6	5	7	3	2	7	

GILGAMESH

Gilgamesh, one of the Eternals, has been known by several names over the centuries, including Hero and the Forgotten One. When demons invaded Earth, Gilgamesh fought alongside Captain America and Thor. He stayed on as an Avenger but died during a fight with Immortus. Gilgamesh was reborn in Brazil with no recollection of his previous life until fellow Eternal Ajak restored his memories.

Gilgamesh is one of the Eternals, a race of god-like beings who rivaled the Asgardians for cosmic power.

VITAL STATS
REAL NAME Unknown
OCCUPATION Warrior, adventurer, monster-slayer
BASE Olympia
HEIGHT 6 ft 5 in (1.95 m)
WEIGHT 260 lbs (118 kg)
EYES Blue
HAIR Black
POWERS Gilgamesh possesses superhuman strength and stamina. He can release cosmic energy through his hands and eyes, and also has the power of flight.
ALLIES Thor, Sersi, Avengers
FOES The Deviants, Blastaar, Kang

A classic costume reinforces Gilgamesh's Eternal nature and shows off his muscles.

Gilgamesh can project energy through his hands and eyes, and needs no other weapons.

COMMON ENEMY
The first time they met, Thor and Gilgamesh fought. They later united against their common enemy, the cosmic Celestials.

POWER RANK	ENERGY PROJECTION	STRENGTH	DURABILITY	FIGHTING SKILL	INTELLIGENCE	SPEED
	6	7	7	4	2	4

GRANDMASTER

The Grandmaster once challenged his brother, the Collector, to a competition, pitting his team of Defenders against the Collector's team of Offenders.

The Grandmaster is an exceptionally powerful cosmic being and Elder of the Universe. He copes with the boredom of a long existence by playing cosmic games. He once created copies of a team called the Squadron Supreme to pit against the Avengers. He also tricked the East and West Coast Avengers into fighting each other so he could capture Lady Death. Death escaped his clutches and banned him and his fellow Elders from her realm.

Grandmaster's mind computes numbers to ten decimal places and contains huge amounts of data.

His body is immune to aging and disease, and he has the ability to regenerate if injured.

VITAL STATS

REAL NAME En Dwi Gast
OCCUPATION Cosmic game player
BASE Mobile
HEIGHT 7 ft 1 in (2.15 m)
WEIGHT 240 lbs (108.75 kg)
EYES Red **HAIR** White
POWERS He is immune to aging, and can travel across the galaxy by thought, levitate, project energy blasts, and rearrange matter on an atomic level.
ALLIES The Collector
FOES Thanos, Avengers

SINISTER GAMES
The Grandmaster once used the Avengers' old enemies, the Squadron Sinister, to attack the Thunderbolts.

ENERGY PROJECTION	STRENGTH	DURABILITY	FIGHTING SKILL	INTELLIGENCE	SPEED	POWER RANK
6	4	7	2	6	7	

G

GRAVITON

When an accident gave researcher Franklin Hall control over gravity, he took the name Graviton and imprisoned his fellow researchers. The Avengers stopped him and banished him to an alternate dimension, but he kept returning with new plans for world conquest. Eventually, aliens followed Graviton to Earth from the dimension in which he had been trapped and he seemingly died trying to stop their invasion. However, he has recently been seen battling the Avengers again.

Graviton was one of the first foes the West Coast Avengers ever fought—and was very nearly the last when his gravity controlling powers came close to destroying the team. Graviton has had a deep hatred of the Avengers ever since.

THE CRUSHER
Graviton's powers allow him to increase the gravity above people, making it impossible for them to move while also crushing them. He has also used his power to access other dimensions.

He can alter gravity to allow himself and those around him to fly.

Graviton's powers have increased dramatically since his first appearance.

VITAL STATS
REAL NAME Franklin Hall
OCCUPATION
Researcher, criminal
BASE Mobile
HEIGHT 6 ft 1 in (1.85 m)
WEIGHT 200 lbs (90.75 kg)
EYES Blue/gray **HAIR** Black
POWERS He has control over gravity which allows him to levitate objects, fly, pin opponents to the ground, and generate force fields and shockwaves.
ALLIES Halflife, Quantum, Zzzax
FOES Thunderbolts, Avengers

POWER RANK	ENERGY PROJECTION	STRENGTH	DURABILITY	FIGHTING SKILL	INTELLIGENCE	SPEED
	7	2	6	2	4	6

GRAVITY

High school student Greg Willis gained his powers in a freak wind storm while on vacation. He was later thought to have died saving some fellow heroes from an exploding battleworld, but in fact he was reborn with extra cosmic powers. Willis eventually gave up these powers to return to Earth and join the Avengers Initiative. He became part of the Heavy Hitters team before falling out with Norman Osborn.

One of Gravity's first serious enemies was called the Black Death, a Super Villain who turned out to be the evil alter ego of his fellow hero, the Greenwich Guardian.

A lightweight costume makes flight and gravity manipulation easier.

VITAL STATS
REAL NAME Greg Willis
OCCUPATION Student
BASE New York City
HEIGHT 5 ft 10 in (1.77 m)
WEIGHT 175 lbs (79.5 kg)
EYES Blue **HAIR** Black
POWERS He possesses a second skin of gravitons that he can use to fly, increase his strength, and affect the speed of objects with a touch.
ALLIES Hank Pym, Wasp, Firebird, Avengers
FOES Black Death, the Stranger

GREEN GIANT
Gravity once fought a villain called Chronok alongside Darkhawk, Dagger, Arana, X-23, Sleepwalker, and Terror.

Gravity's punches are extra powerful because he can manipulate the gravity of his opponent.

ENERGY PROJECTION	STRENGTH	DURABILITY	FIGHTING SKILL	INTELLIGENCE	SPEED	POWER RANK
3	3	2	2	2	2	

GREY GARGOYLE

After spilling chemicals on his hand, French chemist Paul Pierre Duval discovered he could turn anything he touched to stone. He could even turn his own body to stone—and still be able to move! As the Super Villain Grey Gargoyle, he fought Thor and the Avengers before joining the Masters of Evil. Pierre once posed as a sculptor, however his sculptures were victims whom he had turned to stone. He was also a member of the Grim Reaper's Lethal Legion.

The Grey Gargoyle has exceptional strength—more than Spider-Man and many other heroes.

STONE COLD
The Grey Gargoyle's touch can turn someone to stone for up to one hour.

Grey Gargoyle wears gloves to prevent himself from turning others to stone by accident.

He is able to transform himself into movable stone with a touch of his right hand.

VITAL STATS
REAL NAME Paul Pierre Duval
OCCUPATION Criminal, chemist, ex-sculptor
BASE Mobile
HEIGHT 5 ft 11 in (1.80 m)
WEIGHT 175 lbs (79.5 kg) in human form; 750 lbs (340 kg) in stone form
EYES Blue in human form; white in stone form **HAIR** Black in human form; gray in stone form
POWERS He can transform himself into living stone, gaining superhuman strength and durability in the process.
ALLIES Doctor Doom, Masters of Evil
FOES Captain America, Thor, Spider-Man

POWER RANK	ENERGY PROJECTION	STRENGTH	DURABILITY	FIGHTING SKILL	INTELLIGENCE	SPEED
	1	4	5	2	3	2

GRIM REAPER

The Grim Reaper has often fought his brother, Wonder Man, but loyalty made him try to avenge Wonder Man's death.

Eric Williams is Grim Reaper. When his brother Simon (Wonder Man) was believed dead following his first meeting with the Avengers, Eric wanted revenge. He asked the criminal Tinkerer for help and received a deadly scythe. The Grim Reaper attacked the Avengers and only a surprise attack from the Black Panther saved them. Since then, he has fought the team several more times.

Grim Reaper's scythe is a force blaster that rotates to form a shield or buzz-saw.

VITAL STATS
REAL NAME Eric Williams
OCCUPATION Criminal
BASE Mobile
HEIGHT 6 ft 4 in (1.93 m)
WEIGHT 225 lbs (102 kg)
EYES Brown **HAIR** Black
POWERS In place of his right hand, Grim Reaper has a scythe fused to his arm that can fire arcs of energy and induce comas.
ALLIES Man-Ape, Tinkerer, Masters of Evil
FOES Wonder Man, Avengers

FEAR THE REAPER
Grim Reaper once belonged to a villain team named Lethal Legion that was opposed to Norman Osborn when he was Iron Patriot.

ENERGY PROJECTION	STRENGTH	DURABILITY	FIGHTING SKILL	INTELLIGENCE	SPEED	POWER RANK
6	2	2	4	2	2	

GROOT

Groot is part of a race the alien Kree called Floral Colossal. His first visit to Earth saw him attack humanity. However, he later changed his ways and formed a close friendship with Rocket Raccoon after the pair met up in jail. They both joined Star-Lord and the Guardians of the Galaxy when the Universe was threatened by Ultron. It sounds as if he only ever says "I am Groot," but to those who listen closely, his words reveal far, far more.

Groot and Rocket Raccoon are very close friends. The two also work well together in a fight, Groot using his strength and height to help Rocket achieve the best angles to attack.

VITAL STATS

REAL NAME Groot
OCCUPATION Adventurer
BASE Mobile
HEIGHT 23 ft (7.01 m), but is variable
WEIGHT 8,000 lbs (3,629 kg), but is variable
EYES Yellow **HAIR** None
POWERS Groot can alter, expand, or grow his body at will. He is immensely strong and can control trees. He can regrow himself from just a splinter of his previous form.
ALLIES Guardians of the Galaxy, Rocket Raccoon
FOES Thanos, Collector, Mojo

Groot's wooden body is not resistant to fire.

Groot can alter the molecular density of his body, making it extremely tough. He can absorb wood for food.

ALIEN TREE
Groot is the biggest and strongest of the Guardians of the Galaxy. He is also one of the cleverest.

POWER RANK

ENERGY PROJECTION	STRENGTH	DURABILITY	FIGHTING SKILL	INTELLIGENCE	SPEED
3	7	4	4	3	3

HANK PYM

Dr. Henry "Hank" Pym discovered Pym Particles, sub-atomic particles that could change the size of people and objects. He used them to alter his size and became Ant-Man, a founding member of the Avengers. He has used Pym Particles to grow to giant size and taken on various heroic guises. He also formed Avengers A.I., dealing with threats caused by artificial intelligence.

Hank Pym was a founding member of the Avengers together with his then girlfriend, Janet Van Dyne, alias the Wasp. The team was first brought together to combat the schemes of the evil Loki.

HERO OF ALL SIZES
Hank Pym's Super Hero identities include Ant-Man, Giant Man, Yellowjacket, and the Wasp.

Hank's various Super Hero costumes change size when he does.

Hank Pym used his Giant Man identity while part of the Avengers Academy.

VITAL STATS
REAL NAME Dr. Henry "Hank" Pym
OCCUPATION Scientist
BASE Mobile
HEIGHT 6 ft (1.82 m), but is variable
WEIGHT 185 lbs (84 kg), but is variable
EYES Blue **HAIR** Blond
POWERS Hank no longer needs Pym Particles to change size. A scientific genius, he is able to employ his size-changing abilities as part of a number of combat styles.
ALLIES The Vision, Wasp and other Avengers, Reed Richards, Tigra
FOES Ultron, Dimitrios, Norman Osborn

ENERGY PROJECTION	STRENGTH	DURABILITY	FIGHTING SKILL	INTELLIGENCE	SPEED	POWER RANK
6	7	3	3	6	3	

HARDBALL

Roger Brokeridge made a deal with the Super Villain Power Broker to receive super-powers in return for a share of the proceeds from his crimes. However, he was hailed a hero when he appeared to save a girl while attempting to rob a truck. As Hardball, he joined the Avengers: Initiative program. A Hydra secret agent, he left to run a Hydra training camp and was eventually captured and jailed.

Hardball joined Hydra, fighting alongside Scorpion. However he later betrayed Hydra to save his girlfriend, the hero Komodo.

ALL BY MYSELF
When the Hulk returned to Earth and went on a rampage, Hardball found himself alone, facing the Hulk and his Warbound allies.

Hardball can create solid balls of energy around his fists, making his punches very painful.

VITAL STATS
REAL NAME Roger Brokeridge
OCCUPATION Hydra agent
BASE Camp Hammond
HEIGHT 6 ft (1.82 m)
WEIGHT 200 lbs (90.75 kg)
EYES Green
HAIR Blond
POWERS Hardball has the ability to create and throw different types of energy balls.
ALLIES Hydra, Scorpion
FOES Komodo, Avengers

POWER RANK	ENERGY PROJECTION	STRENGTH	DURABILITY	FIGHTING SKILL	INTELLIGENCE	SPEED
	5	3	2	4	3	2

HAWKEYE (CLINT BARTON)

Bullseye once stole Hawkeye's name and identity to join Norman Osborn's Avengers. The move led to a showdown with the enraged real Hawkeye.

At age 14, Clint Barton joined the circus and was taught to fight by Trickshot and the original Swordsman. He decided to become a hero after seeing Iron Man, but was at first mistaken for a criminal. He became a real criminal to impress the Black Widow, then reformed and joined the Avengers as Hawkeye. He died defending Earth from the Kree, but was reborn when the Scarlet Witch remade reality, taking on the roles of Ronin, and then Hawkeye again.

Superb hand-eye coordination gives Hawkeye first-class skill with a bow and arrow.

His light, streamlined costume complements his natural athletic and fighting ability.

VITAL STATS
REAL NAME Clinton "Clint" Barton
OCCUPATION Adventurer
BASE New York City
HEIGHT 6 ft 3 in (1.90 m)
WEIGHT 230 lbs (104.25 kg)
EYES Blue **HAIR** Blond
POWERS Hawkeye is an expert archer, and he often employs a variety of trick arrows in addition to regular ones. His skills are enhanced by the extensive training in martial arts and acrobatics he underwent during his time in the circus.
He is able to aim an arrow perfectly from any angle.
ALLIES Black Widow, Iron Man, Captain America
FOES Bullseye

AIR ARCHERY
Clint's archery skills are often at their deadliest when combined with his amazing acrobatic prowess.

ENERGY PROJECTION	STRENGTH	DURABILITY	FIGHTING SKILL	INTELLIGENCE	SPEED	POWER RANK
2	3	2	7	5	3	

HAWKEYE (KATE BISHOP)

Kate Bishop spent her time helping others. Following an attack in the park, Kate took up extensive martial arts and weapons training. She first met the Young Avengers when they tried to save her from gunmen. After Kate joined the team and fought Kang, Iron Man gave her Hawkeye's bow (the original Hawkeye was thought to be dead) and advised her to take his name. The original Hawkeye later became her mentor.

Much of Kate's equipment was found in the ruins of Avengers Mansion and includes a sword used by the Swordsman, a staff used by Mockingbird, and the original Hawkeye's bow.

VITAL STATS

REAL NAME Katherine "Kate" Elizabeth Bishop
OCCUPATION Student
BASE New York City
HEIGHT 5 ft 5 in (1.65 m)
WEIGHT 120 lbs (54.5 kg)
EYES Blue **HAIR** Black
POWERS Kate is highly skilled in archery, fencing, and martial arts. She originally learned many of these skills as self-defense.
ALLIES Stature, Patriot, Vision, Wiccan, Speed, Hawkeye (Barton)
FOES Kang

Kate uses the original Hawkeye's bow and arrows.

Hawkeye's harness holds two battle staves—extendable poles that convert into different weapons.

NATURALLY BRAVE
Despite her lack of super-powers, Kate helped her teammates fight the powerful, time-traveling Kang.

POWER RANK

ENERGY PROJECTION	STRENGTH	DURABILITY	FIGHTING SKILL	INTELLIGENCE	SPEED
1	2	2	3	3	2

HAZMAT

During her time trapped in Arcade's island arena, Hazmat's containment suit was torn and it looked like she would explode. Reptil took her to a safe distance and, having exploded, she seemed to be able to control her abilities.

Jennifer Takeda is able to project various forms of radiation from her body. Unfortunately, for much of her life, she also gave off deadly radiation and had to wear a protective hazmat containment suit to protect those around her. Thus Hazmat became Jennifer's codename. Kidnapped by the villain Arcade and forced to fight in his island arena, she developed the ability to control the radiation her body emitted, freeing her from having to wear a hazmat suit.

The hazmat suit includes breathing apparatus. It is made of specialized plastic material.

LAST DANCE
While at Avengers Academy, Hazmat started to date Mettle, the only student she couldn't hurt with her radiation owing to his indestructible body.

The containment suit helps Hazmat direct radioactive energy.

VITAL STATS
REAL NAME Jennifer Takeda
OCCUPATION Avengers student
BASE Avengers Compound, Los Angeles
HEIGHT Unrevealed
WEIGHT Unrevealed
EYES Blue **HAIR** Black
POWERS Hazmat can produce deadly radiation. This can range from electromagnetic (EMP) bursts to radioactive blasts. She can control how devastating these are.
ALLIES Avengers, Mettle, Reptil, Runaways
FOES Arcade, Baron Zemo, Damian Hellstrom, X-23

ENERGY PROJECTION	STRENGTH	DURABILITY	FIGHTING SKILL	INTELLIGENCE	SPEED
6	2	2	3	2	2

POWER RANK

HELLCAT

Patsy Walker's teenage years were turned into a comic strip by her mother. Patsy was relieved when the strip finished, but her exposure to the world of comic books had given her a lifelong admiration for Super Heroes. After meeting the newly transformed Beast, Patsy helped him to recover. Later, she accompanied him and the Avengers into the base of an evil corporation where she found Greer Nelson's old Cat costume. Patsy wore the costume to fight alongside the Avengers as Hellcat.

Patsy did not remain with the Avengers team for long. She died while married to the Super Villain Daimon Hellstrom, but Hawkeye and the Thunderbolts rescued her from Hell.

VITAL STATS

REAL NAME Patricia Walker
OCCUPATION Adventurer
BASE Mobile
HEIGHT 5 ft 8 in (1.72 m)
WEIGHT 135 lbs (61.25 kg)
EYES Blue **HAIR** Red
POWERS She has minor psionic abilities and is a skilled acrobat. "Demon sight" allows her to see magical objects or creatures, and she is surrounded by a mystical field that can stop magical attacks. Her costume can be summoned at will and enhances her strength and agility.
ALLIES Beast, Valkyrie, Photon, Black Cat, Firestar
FOES Deathurge, Nicholas Scratch

The retractable claws in Patsy's gloves are also self-firing grappling cables.

Her costume is designed to enhance the natural athletic abilities of the wearer.

DETECTIVE SKILLS
She-Hulk selected Hellcat to be a private eye for her company.

POWER RANK

ENERGY PROJECTION	STRENGTH	DURABILITY	FIGHTING SKILL	INTELLIGENCE	SPEED
1	4	3	5	3	2

HERCULES

Hercules is the son of Zeus, king of the Gods of Olympus. He is known as the Prince of Power and is very fond of fighting, believing it to be a gift to fight both allies and enemies. When the Hulk declared war on the world, Hercules at first sided with him before realizing the Hulk was hell-bent on destruction. He nearly died trying to stop the Hulk and since then has adventured with Amadeus Cho, both of them joining Hank Pym's Avengers.

Hercules once pretended to be Thor to fool the evil Dark Elves. His plan misfired when he accidentally ended up marrying their queen, Alflyse.

Hercules' golden mace is strong enough to survive even direct blows from Thor's hammer.

VITAL STATS
REAL NAME Hercules
OCCUPATION Adventurer
BASE Mobile
HEIGHT 6 ft 5 in (1.95 m)
WEIGHT 325 lbs (147.50 kg)
EYES Blue **HAIR** Dark brown
POWERS Hercules is almost immortal. He is trained in hand-to-hand combat and Ancient Greek wrestling skills. He wields a nearly indestructible golden mace.
ALLIES Amadeus Cho, Hulk, Thor
FOES Pluto, Ares

CHAMPIONS
Hercules, Ghost Rider, Angel, Black Widow, and Iceman teamed up as the Champions of Los Angeles.

ENERGY PROJECTION	STRENGTH	DURABILITY	FIGHTING SKILL	INTELLIGENCE	SPEED	POWER RANK
1	7	6	4	2	2	

HIGH EVOLUTIONARY

Herbert Wyndham was a scientist working at Oxford in the 1930s. He invented a genetic accelerator that could speed up evolution and used it on himself at his base on Wundagore Mountain in the European country of Transia. Wyndham's experiments increased his intellect and gave him amazing powers, but unfortunately drove him insane. He tried to evolve all humanity at once, only to be stopped by the Avengers.

The High Evolutionary came into conflict with the New Warriors after capturing Nova.

VITAL STATS

REAL NAME Herbert Wyndham
OCCUPATION Geneticist, scientist, inventor
BASE Wundagore, Transia
HEIGHT 6 ft 2 in (1.87 m), but is variable
WEIGHT 200 lbs (90.75 kg), but is variable
EYES Brown **HAIR** Brown
POWERS He has highly evolved intelligence and psionic powers, and can alter his size. His armor rebuilds his body when he is injured or ages, making him virtually immortal.
ALLIES Black Knight, Knights of Wundagore, Adam Warlock
FOES Galactus, Man-Beast

The High Evolutionary's telepathic powers are generally undetectable by other mind-readers.

INDECISION
Since first meeting the Avengers, the High Evolutionary has faced them as both friend and foe.

The High Evolutionary once created a counter-Earth on the far side of the Sun.

POWER RANK	ENERGY PROJECTION	STRENGTH	DURABILITY	FIGHTING SKILL	INTELLIGENCE	SPEED
	6	2	7	2	6	2

HOOD

Parker Robbins was just a petty thief until he killed a demon who had links to the Super Villain Dormammu. Robbins took the demon's boots and cloak, which gave him exceptional powers but also pushed him in a darker direction. In a short space of time, he became leader of a vast group of Super Villains. Dormammu granted him more power to kill Doctor Strange but the Hood was stopped by the Avengers. He later became part of Norman's Osborn's sinister Cabal of major villains.

The Hood formed a huge criminal gang that included a number of Super Villains. Following the Hood's arrest, the gang quickly split up.

Robbins took the demon's cloak because he thought it was valuable. Only later did he learn its power.

VITAL STATS

REAL NAME Parker Robbins
OCCUPATION Criminal
BASE Unknown
HEIGHT 5 ft 10 in (1.77 m)
WEIGHT 165 lbs (74.75 kg)
EYES Brown **HAIR** Brown
POWERS The cloak granted him invisibility, the ability to fire energy bolts from his hands, and the power to transform himself into a demon.
ALLIES Norman Osborn, Madame Masque
FOES Avengers, Doctor Strange, Inhumans

NEW POWER
The Hood once collected the Infinity Gems in order to become more powerful.

ENERGY PROJECTION	STRENGTH	DURABILITY	FIGHTING SKILL	INTELLIGENCE	SPEED
4	2	2	3	2	2

POWER RANK

HULK

When Bruce Banner saved Rick Jones' life during the testing of a gamma bomb, he was bombarded by gamma rays. The radiation transformed him into a green-skinned monster whom the soldiers named the Hulk. The Incredible Hulk grows stronger as he gets madder. He is a founding member of the Avengers, but he left when he fell out with his teammates.

When the world over which he ruled was destroyed, the Hulk returned to Earth. He wanted to punish those he felt were responsible, including his old ally Doctor Strange.

VITAL STATS

REAL NAME Robert Bruce Banner
OCCUPATION Scientist, wanderer
BASE Mobile
HEIGHT 7 ft (2.13 m), but is variable
WEIGHT 1,150 lbs (521.75 kg), but is variable
EYES Green
HAIR Dark green
POWERS The Hulk possesses almost limitless strength. He can leap several miles in a single bound and his body heals almost instantly.
ALLIES Rick Jones, Amadeus Cho, the Thing, Betty Ross
FOES Leader, Abomination

The Hulk's size has changed several times since his creation.

A HERO DIVIDED
The Hulk hates his alter ego, the mild-mannered scientist Bruce Banner.

POWER RANK	ENERGY PROJECTION	STRENGTH	DURABILITY	FIGHTING SKILL	INTELLIGENCE	SPEED
	1	7	7	4	6	3

HULKLING

Hulkling has become a key member of the Young Avengers. His shape-changing abilities have proved invaluable to his teammates, especially when they took on the Skrulls during the Skrull invasion of Earth.

For years Teddy Altman thought he was a mutant. However, after joining the Young Avengers as Hulkling he found out that he was not a mutant but an alien! His real mother was the Skrull emperor's daughter and his father was the Kree hero Captain Mar-Vell. Both the Skrull and Kree sent warriors to reclaim their heir but they were tricked, and returned with the Super Skrull disguised as Teddy instead. Hulkling remains on Earth with his teammates.

MISTAKEN IDENTITY
The warrior known as the Super Skrull was sent to bring Teddy "home" to the Skrull Empire. However, he went back himself, disguised as Teddy.

Hulkling's bat-like wings provide balance, speed, and maneuverability during flight.

VITAL STATS
REAL NAME Theodore "Teddy" Altman (original Skrull name Dorrek VIII)
OCCUPATION Student, adventurer
BASE Mobile
HEIGHT Variable
WEIGHT Variable
EYES Variable
HAIR Variable
POWERS Hulkling is a shape-shifter, able to change his form into that of anyone he chooses. He also has superhuman strength.
ALLIES Patriot, Wiccan, Hawkeye (Kate Bishop), Iron Lad, Stature
FOES Super Skrull, Kang

ENERGY PROJECTION	STRENGTH	DURABILITY	FIGHTING SKILL	INTELLIGENCE	SPEED
2	6	6	3	4	3

POWER RANK

HYDRA

Hydra has been one of the world's most notorious and deadly terrorist organizations since it was first created in World War II by Nazi agent Baron Strucker. The Baron saw the organization as a way of gaining power for himself, but over the years many others have taken charge, including Madame Hydra. Hydra seeks to bring chaos and disorder to the world. As a result, Hydra agents have repeatedly clashed with S.H.I.E.L.D. operatives and with the Avengers.

Captain America has been fighting Hydra since World War II. Despite numerous defeats at his hands and also by the Avengers and S.H.I.E.L.D., Hydra always reforms and returns.

VITAL STATS

NAME Hydra
ROLE Terrorist organization
BASE Various
LEADERSHIP High Council (previously Baron Strucker, Gorgon, Madame Hydra, Edgar Lascombe)
POWER Sleeper agents embedded at all levels of society all over the world. Operatives have unarmed combat skills and are highly experienced with advanced weaponry of all kinds, as well as explosives. They are also highly trained in espionage techniques.
ALLIES A.I.M., H.A.M.M.E.R.
FOES Avengers, Nick Fury, S.H.I.E.L.D., Secret Warriors

Supreme Hydra Edgar Lascombe rallies Hydra operatives.

Hydra is named after a many-headed, poisonous monster in Greek myth. If one of its heads was cut off, two more would grow in its place.

THE RELUCTANT ASSASSIN
Spider-Woman (Jessica Drew) was briefly a Hydra agent before rebelling and becoming a hero.

HYPERION

Hyperion was the last survivor of an alien world sent to Earth. He was raised on a parallel Earth, becoming that world's greatest Super Hero. When his Earth was destroyed by a cosmic event, he was saved by scientists belonging to the terrorist organization A.I.M. They pulled him into their reality, hoping to use him in one of their many plots against the Avengers. He was freed by Earth's Mightiest Heroes and went on to join the team.

Hyperion has found a home with the Avengers and has become one of their most powerful members. He has helped the team to battle the Titan Thanos and A.I.M., among other foes.

Hyperion has super-acute hearing and senses.

VITAL STATS

REAL NAME
Marcus Milton
OCCUPATION Hero
BASE Mobile
HEIGHT 6 ft 4 in (1.93 m)
WEIGHT 460 lbs (208.5 kg)
EYES Blue **HAIR** Red-blond
POWERS Hyperion's body collects cosmic energy, turning it into pure power. This gives him superhuman strength, speed, durability, and the power of flight. His vision is so acute he can see the molecular breakdown of reality. He also has atomic vision.
ALLIES The Squadron Supreme, Avengers
FOES Thanos, A.I.M.

WITH THE EXILES
Other versions of Hyperion, from other parallel Earths, have also fought alongside the dimension-hopping team known as the Exiles.

ENERGY PROJECTION	STRENGTH	DURABILITY	FIGHTING SKILL	INTELLIGENCE	SPEED
4	6	7	4	5	5

POWER RANK

IMMORTUS

When the time-traveling Kang grew bored of battling the Avengers, he agreed to become an agent of the Time-Keepers, an alien race from the end of time. Renamed Immortus, he has since been both an ally and an enemy of the Avengers, who have often been drawn into his schemes. He was seemingly killed by the time-traveling children of the Avengers.

Immortus started out as a future version of Kang. However, when he was killed and remade by the Time-Keepers, he and Kang became two separate people —each with a deep hatred of the other.

VITAL STATS
REAL NAME Unknown
OCCUPATION Ruler of Limbo
BASE Limbo, a realm beyond time
HEIGHT 6 ft 3 in (1.90 m)
WEIGHT 230 lbs (104.25 kg)
EYES Green **HAIR** Gray
POWERS Due to his time in Limbo, Immortus does not age and is not susceptible to disease. He can travel easily through time and between dimensions and realities, and is able to take others with him. He is also armed with an arsenal of futuristic weaponry.
ALLIES The Time-Keepers
FOES Kang, Rick Jones, Avengers

He has powers of mind control, and can induce hallucinations in others.

Immortus possesses vast stores of knowledge about time and technology.

CHANGING THE FUTURE
During the Destiny War, Immortus tried to destroy the Avengers but was thwarted by Kang, a past version of himself.

POWER RANK	ENERGY PROJECTION	STRENGTH	DURABILITY	FIGHTING SKILL	INTELLIGENCE	SPEED
	5	2	4	1	4	2

IRON FIST

At nine years old, Danny Rand found the fabled city of K'un-Lun, which his father had visited years earlier. After ten years spent studying martial arts he became K'un-Lun's fighting champion and gained the mystical power of the Iron Fist. He then went to New York seeking to avenge his father's death at the hands of a business partner, but ended up showing mercy. He has also mentored the new Power Man and fought alongside Doctor Strange as part of the Defenders.

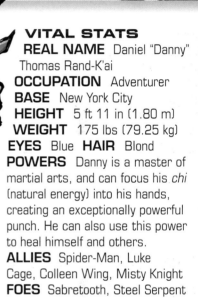

Iron Fist and Luke Cage are close friends who joined the Avengers at the same time. They once worked together as Heroes for Hire.

A dragon tattoo was burned onto his chest during the struggle with the dragon Shou-Lao.

Iron Fist can control his nervous system, dulling his response to pain when in battle.

VITAL STATS

REAL NAME Daniel "Danny" Thomas Rand-K'ai
OCCUPATION Adventurer
BASE New York City
HEIGHT 5 ft 11 in (1.80 m)
WEIGHT 175 lbs (79.25 kg)
EYES Blue **HAIR** Blond
POWERS Danny is a master of martial arts, and can focus his *chi* (natural energy) into his hands, creating an exceptionally powerful punch. He can also use this power to heal himself and others.
ALLIES Spider-Man, Luke Cage, Colleen Wing, Misty Knight
FOES Sabretooth, Steel Serpent

FIRE FIGHTING
Danny gained the power of the Iron Fist by defeating the dragon Shou-Lao the Undying. To do this, he had to plunge his hands into the flames that guarded the dragon's molten heart.

ENERGY PROJECTION	STRENGTH	DURABILITY	FIGHTING SKILL	INTELLIGENCE	SPEED	POWER RANK
3	2	3	6	3	2	

IRON LAD

Nathaniel Richards lived in the 31st century. When he was 16, his future self, Kang, travelled through time to save him from a vicious bully. Nathaniel was shocked to see the dictator he was destined to become, and was desperate to change the course of his future. He travelled back to the present day to seek help from the Avengers, but they had just been defeated by the Scarlet Witch. So, calling himself Iron Lad, Nathaniel formed the Young Avengers to defeat his future self.

Nathaniel escaped to the present day with a psychokinetic suit of armor given to him by his future self, Kang the Conqueror. He based his appearance on that of Iron Man, his hero from the Avengers.

VITAL STATS
REAL NAME Nathaniel Richards
OCCUPATION Student
BASE New York City
HEIGHT 5 ft 9 in (1.75 m)
WEIGHT 166 lbs (75.25 kg)
EYES Brown **HAIR** Brown
POWERS Iron Lad's futuristic armor obeys his every thought and can hack into any computer system. It can also emit various force fields and gives him the power of flight.
ALLIES Patriot, Hulkling, Wiccan, Stature, Hawkeye (Kate Bishop)
FOES Kang, Super Skrull

Iron Lad's armor can emit energy blasts, magnetic fields, and fire-extinguishing foam.

Armor contains an internal hard drive on which vast amounts of data can be stored.

HERO'S CHOICE
Iron Lad was eventually forced to go back to his own time in order to save the lives of his friends in the Young Avengers.

POWER RANK	ENERGY PROJECTION	STRENGTH	DURABILITY	FIGHTING SKILL	INTELLIGENCE	SPEED
	6	4	5	3	4	2

IRON MAN

Billionaire businessman Tony Stark is one of the most intelligent and influential people on the planet. While testing weaponry in Vietnam, he was caught in an explosion and captured by the warlord Wong-Chu. With a piece of shrapnel lodged dangerously near to his heart, Tony created the first set of Iron Man armor to aid his escape and ensure his survival. He was a founding member of the Avengers and wants to make the world a better place.

Tony Stark was originally involved in the creation of high-tech weapons. He often helped the armed forces, once even becoming U.S. Secretary of Defense.

VITAL STATS
REAL NAME Anthony "Tony" Stark
OCCUPATION Businessman
BASE Stark Tower, New York City
HEIGHT 6 ft 1 in (1.85 m)
WEIGHT 225 lbs (102 kg)
EYES Blue **HAIR** Black
POWERS Standard Iron Man armour provides exceptional strength, speed, and the power of flight. Repulsor beams in the gauntlets and the uni-beam in the chest piece can also be used. He has many other sets of armor for special missions.
ALLIES Black Widow, Mr. Fantastic, War Machine
FOES Mandarin, Iron Patriot, Iron Monger

The uni-beam emits light particles and electron beams as a spotlight or laser weapon.

The palm repulsor rays block incoming attacks and utilize electron beams to amplify force.

GLOBAL INTERFACING
Tony Stark is constantly upgrading his armour. He recently gained the power to talk directly to computers across the world.

ENERGY PROJECTION	STRENGTH	DURABILITY	FIGHTING SKILL	INTELLIGENCE	SPEED	POWER RANK
6	6	6	3	6	5	

IRON PATRIOT

James Rhodes is one of the few people other than Tony Stark to wear the Iron Man armor. He first put it on when Stark was ill and out of action. When Stark returned to the role, Rhodes became War Machine. He fought with the Avengers both as Iron Man and as War Machine. At the request of the U.S. military, he then used modified Iron Man armor to become the latest Iron Patriot, helping to pacify several suits of armour that had gained sentience.

As War Machine, James Rhodes fought alongside his friend Iron Man several times, teaming up with him to defeat foes such as the Melter, the Iron Monger (Obadiah Stane), and the Mandarin.

VITAL STATS
REAL NAME James Rhodes
OCCUPATION
Super Hero, soldier
BASE Mobile
HEIGHT 6 ft 6 in (1.98 m)
WEIGHT 210 lbs (95.25 kg)
EYES Blue **HAIR** Black
POWERS Rhodes has no super-powers but is a trained U.S. Marine and an experienced pilot with a strong working knowledge of Iron Man armor.
ALLIES Avengers, Tony Stark, U.S. Marine Corps
FOES Mandarin, Norman Osborn

Helmet features a breathing apparatus to facilitate space travel.

The Iron Patriot armor houses various concealed high-tech weapons.

MARK 1
Norman Osborn was the original Iron Patriot, modifying an old suit of Iron Man's armor for the role.

	ENERGY PROJECTION	STRENGTH	DURABILITY	FIGHTING SKILL	INTELLIGENCE	SPEED
POWER RANK	6	6	6	4	3	5

JACK OF HEARTS

Jack Hart's father was a scientist and inventor of a new energy source—Zero Fluid. Jack gained amazing powers after he became covered in the fluid when thieves killed his father. He avenged the murder, then took the name Jack of Hearts in memory of his father's love of playing cards. Jack later joined the Avengers, but was killed while rescuing Ant-Man's (Scott Lang's) daughter.

Jack nearly killed the alien armorer, Torvail, when they first met. Torvail still helped him, upgrading his armor.

The left side of Jack's body was bluish-purple, a result of his mother's alien origins.

Jack wore special armor to contain his destructive energy.

VITAL STATS
REAL NAME Jonathan "Jack" Hart
OCCUPATION Adventurer
BASE Mobile
HEIGHT 5 ft 11 in (1.80 m)
WEIGHT 175 lbs (79.25 kg)
EYES Blue (right), white (left)
HAIR Brown
POWERS Jack had enhanced strength, rapid healing, and the ability to release massive amounts of explosive energy. He could also fly and travel though space.
ALLIES Iron Man, Spider-Man
FOES Simon Maris, Pagan, Kree

FOR THE CURE
Ant-Man tried to cure Jack of his unwanted deadly powers. His efforts often resulted in heated arguments.

ENERGY PROJECTION	STRENGTH	DURABILITY	FIGHTING SKILL	INTELLIGENCE	SPEED	POWER RANK
5	4	6	3	4	7	

JARVIS

Jarvis is the heart of the Avengers. The former R.A.F. pilot and war hero was Tony Stark's parents' butler and, after their deaths, looked after Tony. When the family mansion became the Avengers' base, Jarvis began working for the team. He is often drawn into their adventures, and has been brainwashed by Ultron into attacking the Avengers as well as being replaced by a Skrull imposter.

Jarvis is far more than just a butler to the Avengers. He is a friend and confidant to old and new members alike, and is the only non-Avenger team member to live on the premises.

VITAL STATS
REAL NAME Edwin Jarvis
OCCUPATION Butler
BASE Mobile
HEIGHT 5 ft 11 in (1.80 m)
WEIGHT 160 lbs (72.5 kg)
EYES Blue **HAIR** Black
POWERS Jarvis is a former boxing champion and pilot. He is resourceful and calm under pressure, making him an ideal person to dispense advice. His organization and management skills are highly useful. Jarvis is also a world authority on removing otherworldly stains from furniture and carpets.
ALLIES Avengers
FOES Ultron, Skrulls

As well as his other skills, Jarvis is an ace with a vacuum cleaner.

FINANCIAL CONTROLLER
Jarvis controls the Avengers' finances and organizes the housekeeping of Avengers Mansion.

	ENERGY PROJECTION	STRENGTH	DURABILITY	FIGHTING SKILL	INTELLIGENCE	SPEED
POWER RANK	1	2	2	3	3	2

JESSICA JONES

Teenager Jessica Jones was exposed to radioactive chemicals and became the Super Hero Jewel. The Purple Man forced her to attack the Avengers and she was left in a coma until Jean Grey of the X-Men revived her. After this, Jessica gave up the Super Hero life and became a journalist and later a detective. During the Secret Invasion, her baby was kidnapped by a Skrull pocing as the Avengers' butler, Jarvis. Jessica's husband, Luke Cage, rescued her with help from Norman Osborn.

Jewel once put on her old Super Hero uniform to confront the Young Avengers.

Her sharp mind and excellent memory enhance her skills as a detective and reporter.

Jessica got her powers after a car crash brought her into contact with a cylinder of experimental chemicals.

VITAL STATS
REAL NAME Jessica Jones
OCCUPATION Private investigator, journalist
BASE New York City
HEIGHT 5 ft 7 in (1.70 m)
WEIGHT 124 lbs (56.25 kg)
EYES Brown **HAIR** Brown
POWERS Jessica possesses the powers of flight, superhuman strength, and a high resistance to injury.
ALLIES Luke Cage, Spider-Man, Clay Quartermain, Captain Marvel (Carol Danvers)
FOES Purple Man, Norman Osborn, Owl

HAPPY FAMILY
Jessica and Luke Cage are the proud parents of a baby girl, who is adored by many of their fellow heroes.

ENERGY PROJECTION	STRENGTH	DURABILITY	FIGHTING SKILL	INTELLIGENCE	SPEED	POWER RANK
1	4	4	3	2		

JOCASTA

Ultron, the robotic enemy of the Avengers, created the robot Jocasta to be his mate. He based her personality on the original Wasp, the wife of Ultron's creator, Hank Pym. However, Jocasta rebelled against Ultron. She helped the Avengers defeat her creator and joined the team for a while. After spending time with Hank Pym's Avengers team, she became a teacher at the Avengers Academy.

During the Skrull Invasion, Jocasta fought the invaders with Devil-Slayer and her fellow Initiative members in New Mexico.

ROBOT HUNTER
Jocasta helped the Avengers A.I. team, creating a squad of robotic hunters to help the team track their enemies.

The energy blasts emitted from Jocasta's red, glowing eyes are a powerful—and intimidating—weapon.

Her titanium steel shell provides resistance to nearly all forms of physical damage.

VITAL STATS
REAL NAME Jocasta
OCCUPATION Former adventurer, computer
BASE Mobile
HEIGHT 5 ft 9 in (1.75 m)
WEIGHT 750 lbs (340.25 kg)
EYES Red **HAIR** None
POWERS Jocasta possesses a superhuman ability to process information, as well as superhuman strength and endurance. She can blast energy from hands and eyes.
ALLIES Wasp (Hank Pym), Vision, Machine Man
FOES Ultron

POWER RANK	ENERGY PROJECTION	STRENGTH	DURABILITY	FIGHTING SKILL	INTELLIGENCE	SPEED
	3	4	6	2	4	2

JUSTICE

Vance Astrovik was a teenager when his mutant telekinetic abilities were revealed during a meeting with his future self, Vance Astro. This altered the course of Vance's future and, calling himself Marvel Boy, he joined the New Warriors with Night Thrasher, Nova, and Firestar. Vance later changed his name to Justice and became a member of the Avengers.

For a time, Justice and Firestar were engaged to be married. They were both reserve members of the Avengers before becoming part of the new line-up.

Justice has a vast, encyclopedic knowledge about Super Heroes.

Justice's aerodynamic costume allows movement and flight with minimal air resistance.

NEW WARRIORS
Justice reformed the New Warriors with Speedball. They were joined by Nova, Scarlet Spider, Haechi, Water Snake, and Hummingbird.

VITAL STATS
REAL NAME Vance Astrovik
OCCUPATION Adventurer
BASE Mobile
HEIGHT 5 ft 10 in (1.77 m)
WEIGHT 180 lbs (81.75 kg)
EYES Hazel **HAIR** Brown
POWERS A mutant with strong telekinetic abilities, Vance can move objects using only his mind, and can send mental blasts at his enemies. He can also use his powers to make himself and others fly.
ALLIES Firestar, Speedball, Rage
FOES Nitro, Norman Osborn

ENERGY PROJECTION	STRENGTH	DURABILITY	FIGHTING SKILL	INTELLIGENCE	SPEED	POWER RANK
5	2	5	3	3	3	

KANG

Nathaniel Richards discovered time travel, and journeyed back from his own timeline in 3000 CE to Ancient Egypt. There he ruled as Rama Tut for several years, later traveling to the 40th century where he created an empire as Kang the Conqueror. Kang is usually an enemy of the Avengers, but once joined forces with them to prevent his future self, Immortus, from wiping out a number of parallel worlds.

Kang traveled back in time to bring his younger self, Iron Lad, back to the present. But Iron Lad formed the Young Avengers in the hope of never becoming Kang.

His suit has a self-contained atmosphere, food supply, and waste disposal system.

VITAL STATS

REAL NAME
Nathaniel Richards
OCCUPATION Conqueror
BASE Mobile
HEIGHT 6 ft 3 in (1.90 m)
WEIGHT 230 lbs (104.25 kg)
EYES Brown **HAIR** Brown
POWERS He is a master of time travel. His suit provides super strength and protection. He has access to future weapons.
ALLIES Parallel/alternate Kangs
FOES Hulkling, Ravonna, Avengers

Kang has instant access to a vast array of highly advanced weapons.

OVER AND OVER AGAIN
The time-traveling conqueror Kang has fought the Avengers in many different timelines.

His body armor can lift 5 tons (4.5 tonnes) and project a defensive force field.

POWER RANK	ENERGY PROJECTION	STRENGTH	DURABILITY	FIGHTING SKILL	INTELLIGENCE	SPEED
	1	3	3	4	4	7

KA-ZAR

Lord Robert Plunder was killed by human-like beings called Man-Apes while in the Savage Land, a lost realm hidden beneath Antarctica. His young son, Kevin, nearly died, too, but was saved by a saber-toothed tiger called Zabu. Kevin grew up to become a legendary warrior whom the natives named Ka-Zar, and married Shanna the She-Devil. The couple has fought alongside the Avengers many times, including when the Skrulls invaded.

Ka-Zar lives in the Savage Land, a lost realm where dinosaurs still exist alongside cavemen, and a variety of strange races dwell. It was originally set up as a kind of game preserve by aliens called the Beyonders, who wanted to observe evolution in action.

SAVAGE LAND TEAM-UPS
Wolverine, Spidey, and their allies have often teamed up with Ka-Zar when their adventures have taken them to the Savage Land.

Ka-Zar has an empathy with wild animals and is expert at handling them.

The name Ka-Zar means "Son of the Tiger" in the language of the Man-Apes.

VITAL STATS

REAL NAME Lord Kevin Plunder
OCCUPATION Hunter, Lord of the Savage Land
BASE The Savage Land
HEIGHT 6 ft 2 in (1.87 m)
WEIGHT 215 lbs (97.5 kg)
EYES Blue **HAIR** Blond
POWERS A hunting, combat, and survival expert, Ka-Zar excels in hand-to-hand combat, and the use of the bow and arrow, spear, and sling.
ALLIES Shanna the She-Devil, Zabu, Wolverine, Spider-Man, Namor, the Sub-Mariner
FOES Parnival the Plunderer, Thanos

ENERGY PROJECTION	STRENGTH	DURABILITY	FIGHTING SKILL	INTELLIGENCE	SPEED	POWER RANK
1	3	2	5	2	3	

KLAW

Ulysses Klaw was developing a device to turn sound into physical objects and tried to steal Vibranium from Wakanda to help him. He failed, and lost his hand in the attempt. Finally obtaining Vibranium on the black market, Klaw created a sonic blaster to replace his hand. Later, faced with defeat by the Black Panther, Klaw threw himself into a sonic converter and was transformed into living sound. He has often fought the Black Panther and the Avengers.

Klaw was part of a formidable version of the Masters of Evil, teaming up with the Melter, Whirlwind, and the Radioactive Man. His mission was to take revenge on the Black Panther and the Avengers.

VITAL STATS

REAL NAME Ulysses Klaw
OCCUPATION Scientist, criminal
BASE Mobile
HEIGHT 5 ft 11 in (1.80 m)
WEIGHT 175 lbs (79.25 kg)
EYES Red **HAIR** None
POWERS Klaw can turn sounds into objects and reshape his body, which is made of sound waves. He can also project deafening blasts and sound waves from his blaster.
ALLIES Solarr, Doctor Demonicus
FOES Black Panther, Fantastic Four, Avengers

A blaster replaces the hand that was destroyed when the Black Panther used Klaw's own weapon against him.

His body requires no food or water and can reform itself even after complete destruction.

MASTER OF SOUND
Klaw is the Master of Sound and the sound waves from his blaster can stop enemies as strong as Ms. Marvel.

POWER RANK	ENERGY PROJECTION	STRENGTH	DURABILITY	FIGHTING SKILL	INTELLIGENCE	SPEED
	5	4	7	4	4	4

KOMODO

Melati Kusuma lost both her legs in a car accident and wanted to restore them. She used a version of Doctor Curt Connors' regenerative formula on herself without permission and it transformed her into a lizard woman. Taking on the name Komodo, Melati joined the Avengers Initiative. After leaving, she worked with Jeremy Briggs, not realizing he was a Super Villain.

While part of the Initiative, Komodo accompanied the Shadow Initiative to the island of Madripoor to bring her ex-teammate Hardball (a secret Hydra agent) to justice. Komodo was taken prisoner by Hydra, but the Shadow Initiative later freed her.

SPIDER-CATCHER
In New York, Komodo found herself trying to bring Spider-Man to justice for refusing to sign the Super Hero Registration Act.

Komodo's claws give an added edge to her superhuman strength.

In her lizard form, Melati's legs are fully restored.

VITAL STATS
REAL NAME Melati Kusuma
OCCUPATION Adventurer
BASE Arizona
HEIGHT Variable
WEIGHT Variable
EYES Black **HAIR** Black
POWERS In her lizard woman form, she has superhuman strength, speed, and endurance, plus armored skin, sharpened teeth and claws, and a quick healing factor.
ALLIES MVP
FOES Spider-Man, Hardball, Hydra

ENERGY PROJECTION	STRENGTH	DURABILITY	FIGHTING SKILL	INTELLIGENCE	SPEED	POWER RANK
1	3	4	3	2	3	

KORVAC

Korvac is a computer technician from 2997 CE. When alien Badoon invaders found him asleep at work, they punished him by grafting a computer to his lower body. He was transported to the present day by the Grandmaster, who wanted to make use of him. However, Korvac downloaded some of Grandmaster's powers, then stole some of Galactus' powers. He became one of the most powerful beings in existence, able to remake reality itself.

Even the combined might of the Avengers wasn't enough to stop Korvac.

ULTIMATE POWER
Korvac planned to alter reality and bring about a perfect world.

Korvac has a cyborg body and a brain that can analyze data about his foes and respond almost instantly.

VITAL STATS
REAL NAME Michael Korvac
OCCUPATION Computer technician, would-be Master of the Universe
BASE Mobile
HEIGHT 6 ft 3 in (1.90 m)
WEIGHT Unrevealed
EYES Blue **HAIR** Blond
POWERS Cosmic powers on a vast scale, including the ability to time travel, fly, and mask his presence so he seems invisible.
ALLIES Carina
FOES Avengers, Guardians of the Galaxy, Galactus

He can project deadly energy blasts from his hands.

POWER RANK

ENERGY PROJECTION	STRENGTH	DURABILITY	FIGHTING SKILL	INTELLIGENCE	SPEED
7	7	7	2	7	7

LIONHEART

At first Kelsey was unable to reveal her powers to her children, but she reunited with them when she returned to England. As Lionheart, Kelsey helped out the Excalibur Super Hero team, led by Brian Braddock.

Teacher Kelsey Leigh gave her life to protect Captain America from the Wrecking Crew Super Villain team. She was given a second chance to live by the spirit of Brian Braddock, the former Captain Britain, who gave her the Sword of Might and made her his successor. Kelsey joined the Avengers and helped them defeat Morgan Le Fay. She later changed her name to Lionheart and continued her Super Hero career in England.

Lionheart can generate a powerful force field to protect herself from attack.

VITAL STATS
REAL NAME Kelsey Leigh
OCCUPATION Adventurer
BASE England
HEIGHT 5 ft 5 in (1.65 m)
WEIGHT 130 lbs (59 kg)
EYES Blue **HAIR** Blonde
POWERS She has superhuman strength and reactions. The Sword of Might allows her to project energy blasts. She can also fly.
ALLIES Captain Britain, Captain America
FOES Morgan Le Fay, Mordred, Albion

The Sword of Might sends out blasts of energy which can disarm enemies and also act as a shield.

AVENGER
As Captain Britain, Kelsey was a member of the Avengers for a time. She saved Captain America once more, this time from She-Hulk.

ENERGY PROJECTION	STRENGTH	DURABILITY	FIGHTING SKILL	INTELLIGENCE	SPEED
4	6	5	4	3	4

POWER RANK

LIVING LASER

Arthur Parks was a scientist who created small but powerful lasers. He fixed the lasers to his wrists and embarked on a life of crime as the Living Laser.
Early in his career he was obsessed with the Wasp and kidnapped her. This brought him into conflict with the Avengers, who defeated him.
He was also part of the Masters of Evil, and later had his abilities upgraded by the Mandarin to help him fight Iron Man.

The Living Laser's human body was destroyed when his lasers overloaded and exploded during a battle with Iron Man. Parks kept his human consciousness but is now made up entirely of photons (light energy), and is more powerful than ever.

VITAL STATS

REAL NAME Arthur Parks
OCCUPATION Criminal
BASE Mobile
HEIGHT Not applicable; was 5 ft 11 in (1.80 m) in human form
WEIGHT Not applicable; was 185 lbs (84 kg) in human form
EYES Blue **HAIR** Brown
POWERS Composed of light, Living Laser can travel at light speed or transform himself into an offensive weapon. He can also create targeted holographic images.
ALLIES M.O.D.O.K., Hood, Mandarin
FOES Avengers, Iron Man

M.O.D.O.K.'S 11
M.O.D.O.K. selected Living Laser to be a member of his team of criminals, M.O.D.O.K.'s 11.

By adjusting the density of his photons, Living Laser creates the illusion of a physical body.

	ENERGY PROJECTION	STRENGTH	DURABILITY	FIGHTING SKILL	INTELLIGENCE	SPEED
POWER RANK	5	4	7	2	4	6

LIVING LIGHTNING

Miguel Santos' father led the Legion of Living Lightning Super Villain group, and Miguel planned to follow in his footsteps. However, an accident in the Legion's base transformed Miguel into a being of pure energy—Living Lightning. The Super Villain Demonicus gave him a suit to control his power, but when he faced the Avengers, Miguel switched sides, turning against him.

The Legion of Living Lightning wanted to overthrow the U.S. government. Miguel's father Carlos was killed, along with most of the Legion, when their attempt to control the Hulk went wrong.

GRADUATE
After turning his back on evil, Miguel became a member of the West Coast Avengers.

Miguel can create lightning bolts and control electronics.

This containment suit controls the pure energy within and maintains Miguel's human form.

VITAL STATS
REAL NAME Miguel Santos
OCCUPATION Student
BASE Texas
HEIGHT 5 ft 9 in (1.75 m)
WEIGHT 170 lbs (77 kg)
EYES Brown **HAIR** Black
POWERS Miguel can transform his body into electricity and use it to attack enemies or to fly.
ALLIES Avengers, Photon, Quasar
FOES Demonicus, Magus

ENERGY PROJECTION	STRENGTH	DURABILITY	FIGHTING SKILL	INTELLIGENCE	SPEED
4	2	5	4	2	6

POWER RANK

LOCKJAW

Lockjaw is an Inhuman dog-like creature with powers of teleportation. He helped the Inhumans locate their leader Black Bolt when Black Bolt was kidnapped by the Skrulls. He is extremely protective of his friends. Lockjaw's intelligence was increased by one of the Infinity Gems and he formed the Pet Avengers to locate the other gems, defeating Thanos along the way.

Lockjaw is the leader of the Pet Avengers animal Super Hero team. His teammates include Zabu, a sabertoothed tiger, Redwing, a falcon, and Lockheed, a dragon.

VITAL STATS
REAL NAME Unrevealed
OCCUPATION Adventurer
BASE Attilan
HEIGHT 6 ft 8 in (2.03 m)
WEIGHT 1,240 lbs (562.5 kg)
EYES Brown **HAIR** Brown
POWERS Lockjaw has exceptional physical strength and can teleport himself across space and parallel dimensions. When teleporting, he can take up to 12 others who touch him along for the ride.
ALLIES Black Bolt, Zabu, Redwing, Lockheed
FOES Doctor Doom, Thanos

Lockjaw's immensely strong jaw is a fearsome weapon.

His intimidating size and weight scares enemies and boosts his physical strength.

ANY DESTINATION...
Lockjaw uses his powers to teleport members of the Inhuman royal family wherever they desire to go.

POWER RANK

	ENERGY PROJECTION	STRENGTH	DURABILITY	FIGHTING SKILL	INTELLIGENCE	SPEED
	5	5	5	4	2	5

LOKI

Loki is the Norse god of evil and the son of Laufey, king of the Frost Giants. When the Asgardians defeated the Frost Giants, the Asgardian king, Odin, took Loki to Asgard and raised him as his own son. Loki died protecting Asgard but was reincarnated as a boy, later using magic to transform himself into a teenager. Whether this new Loki is evil remains to be seen.

Loki was still in the guise of a young boy when he joined the Young Avengers, but he manipulated Wiccan to transform him into a teenager, thereby increasing his own powers.

BATTLING BROTHERS
Loki and Thor share a long sibling rivalry. One attempt by Loki to kill Thor ultimately led to the formation of the Avengers.

Although he has a distinctive costume, Loki can assume the appearance of anyone he chooses.

VITAL STATS
REAL NAME Loki Laufeyson
OCCUPATION God of evil
BASE Asgard
HEIGHT 6 ft 4 in (1.93 m)
WEIGHT 525 lbs (238.25 kg)
EYES Green **HAIR** Gray/black
POWERS With enhanced strength and stamina, Loki is all but immortal. He has an exceptional knowledge of sorcery and uses it to fly, change shape, teleport, and move between dimensions.
ALLIES The Enchantress, Norman Osborn
FOES Thor, Avengers, Balder the Brave

ENERGY PROJECTION	STRENGTH	DURABILITY	FIGHTING SKILL	INTELLIGENCE	SPEED	POWER RANK
6	5	6	3	5	7	

LUKE CAGE

Carl Lucas was set up by his friend William Stryker and jailed for a crime he didn't commit. While in jail, Lucas took part in a cell-regeneration experiment that accidentally increased his strength and gave him bulletproof skin. He used his new strength to break out of jail, took on the name Luke Cage, and became a Hero for Hire. Luke later joined the New Avengers and later formed his own team of Mighty Avengers.

Luke joined Iron Fist to form a new version of the Heroes for Hire. The line-up included ex-Avengers Hulk and Black Knight.

Luke Cage is married to Jessica Jones, who is also known as Jewel.

Luke Cage's impenetrable skin deflects bullets, resists blades, and is impervious to electricity.

VITAL STATS

REAL NAME Carl Lucas
OCCUPATION Bodyguard, private investigator
BASE New York City
HEIGHT 6 ft 6 in (1.98 m)
WEIGHT 425 lbs (192.75 kg)
EYES Brown **HAIR** Black
POWERS He has superhuman strength and steel-hard skin. He recovers quickly from injury and is a skilled street fighter.
ALLIES Jessica Jones, Iron Fist, Fantastic Four
FOES Gideon Mace, Diamondback

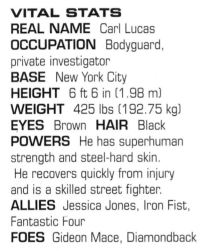

LUKE'S AVENGERS
Luke's "Mighty Avengers" team included White Tiger, Power Man, Spectrum, and Spider-Man. Later, Iron Fist and Blue Marvel also joined.

POWER RANK	ENERGY PROJECTION	STRENGTH	DURABILITY	FIGHTING SKILL	INTELLIGENCE	SPEED
	1	4	5	4	3	2

Machine Man and Jocasta were once sent on a mission to a parallel world where a virus had turned everyone with super-powers into zombies. As machines, they were both immune to the virus.

MACHINE MAN

M

Machine Man (a.k.a. X-51) was the last of 51 robots Dr. Abel Stack created for the army. Stack kept X-51 for himself and treated him like a son. When the other robots malfunctioned and were ordered to self destruct, Stack removed Machine Man's self-destruct mechanism, but somehow triggered it and was killed. X-51 went on the run, wearing a rubber mask and taking the name Aaron Stack. He fell in love with Jocasta of the Avengers and became a reserve team member.

Telescoping arms and legs provide immediate advantage over foes.

VITAL STATS
REAL NAME X-51/Aaron Stack
OCCUPATION Adventurer, secret agent
BASE Mobile
HEIGHT 6 ft (1.82 m)
WEIGHT 850 lbs (376.50 kg)
EYES Red **HAIR** Black
POWERS He has extendable limbs, weapons built into his body, the ability to fly, and super-strength.
ALLIES Jocasta, Photon
FOES Ultron, Fin Fang Foom

IN BITS
Machine Man was once forced to rebuild his body from spare bits of machinery after almost being destroyed.

X-51 has concealed weapons in his fingers and elsewhere in his armor.

ENERGY PROJECTION	STRENGTH	DURABILITY	FIGHTING SKILL	INTELLIGENCE	SPEED
6	4	6	4	4	3

POWER RANK

107

MADAME HYDRA

Ophelia Sarkissian was born in Hungary. Her parents died during a revolution and Ophelia was attacked and left scarred. She grew up living on her wits, becoming a mercenary known as Viper. She joined Hydra and quickly rose to prominence, taking the name Madame Hydra and launching several terrorist attacks. She seeks to destroy a world she hates. She has learned how to kill from some of the world's deadliest teachers and is a woman that many have learned to fear.

Madame Hydra joined forces with Norman Osborn and A.I.M. scientists, creating modified versions of the Hulk out of Hydra agents to use against the Avengers.

Madame Hydra conceals her scarred face with her hair.

SUPREME COUNCIL
Madame Hydra joined forces with other villains to attack Spider-Man and the Avengers.

She has modified her canine teeth to contain toxins; her bite is deadly.

VITAL STATS
REAL NAME Ophelia Sarkissian
OCCUPATION Professional criminal
BASE Mobile
HEIGHT 5 ft 9 in (1.75 m)
WEIGHT 140 lbs (63.5 kg)
EYES Green
HAIR Black (usually dyed green)
POWERS Trained in a variety of martial arts and espionage tactics, Madame Hydra is experienced with numerous weapons but favors whips and knives.
ALLIES Baron Zemo, Norman Osborn, Silver Samurai
FOES Avengers, Nick Fury

POWER RANK	ENERGY PROJECTION	STRENGTH	DURABILITY	FIGHTING SKILL	INTELLIGENCE	SPEED
	1	3	2	6	3	

MADAME MASQUE

Countess Giulietta Nefaria grew up as Whitney Frost, unaware that she was really the daughter of the master criminal Count Nefaria. After her adoptive father died, Count Nefaria revealed Giulietta's true identity and she joined him in the Maggia criminal organization. Her face was scarred during a botched raid on Stark Industries so she started wearing a golden mask and adopted the name Madame Masque.

Madame Masque has faced the Avengers many times and fought alongside the Hood's group of Super Villains.

Giulietta's mask is so strong that bullets simply bounce off it, causing her no serious injury.

The golden mask hides severe chemical burn scars.

VITAL STATS
REAL NAME Countess Giulietta Nefaria
OCCUPATION Head of Maggia criminal organization
BASE Mobile
HEIGHT 5 ft 9 in (1.75 m)
WEIGHT 130 lbs (59 kg)
EYES Gray **HAIR** Black
POWERS An excellent markswoman and keen strategist, Giulietta is also an Olympic-level gymnast and athlete.
ALLIES Count Nefaria, Hood, Midas
FOES Iron Man, Avengers

CLONE CREATOR
Countess Nefaria has created many clones of herself. One, called Masque, joined the Avengers and died fighting alongside them.

ENERGY PROJECTION	STRENGTH	DURABILITY	FIGHTING SKILL	INTELLIGENCE	SPEED	POWER RANK
1	2	2	4	3	2	

MAN-APE

M'Baku was one of Wakanda's greatest warriors. When the Black Panther became a member of the Avengers, M'Baku attempted to take over Wakanda. He revived the outlawed White Gorilla cult, killing one of the beasts to gain its power and taking the name Man-Ape before challenging the Black Panther. He tried to take over Wakanda several times but was eventually killed by Spider-Man's enemy, Morlun, who drained his life-force.

While Man-Ape and the Black Panther were rivals, they also respected each other. Black Panther invited Man-Ape to his wedding and Man-Ape warned the Panther of a threat to his life.

WHITE AND BLACK
Man-Ape's ferocity and power, gained from the White Gorilla cult, rivaled the strength of Black Panther.

As leader of the White Gorilla Cult, Man-Ape had exceptional strength.

Man-Ape wore the hide of the white gorilla he killed.

VITAL STATS
REAL NAME M'Baku
OCCUPATION Mercenary
BASE Wakanda
HEIGHT 7 ft (2.13 m)
WEIGHT 355 lbs (161 kg)
EYES Brown **HAIR** Brown
POWERS Man-Ape possessed superhuman strength, speed, stamina, and resistance to injury. His powers were gained from eating the flesh and bathing in the blood of of a sacred white gorilla, and his fighting abilities were based on those of a gorilla.
ALLIES Grim Reaper, Masters of Evil
FOES Black Panther, Avengers, Henry Peter Gyrich

POWER RANK	ENERGY PROJECTION	STRENGTH	DURABILITY	FIGHTING SKILL	INTELLIGENCE	SPEED
	1	4	3	4	2	3

MANDARIN

Both Iron Man and War Machine (Jim Rhodes, later known as Iron Patriot) have fought the Mandarin. In one of their greatest battles a rejuvenated Mandarin created his own city and came close to killing both heroes.

A brilliant scientist and expert martial artist, the Mandarin is Iron Man's archenemy. The Mandarin was born in 1920 to a wealthy Chinese family and can trace his ancestry back to Genghis Khan. His main source of power comes from ten alien rings that he found in a crashed spaceship. These grant him amazing abilities. While he has seemingly died several times, he has always returned—stronger and more powerful than ever.

The Mandarin has used his alien, sentient rings to rejuvenate his body.

VITAL STATS

REAL NAME Unknown, possibly Khan
OCCUPATION Criminal mastermind
BASE The Palace of the Star Dragon in the Valley of Spirits, China
HEIGHT 6 ft 2 in (1.88 m)
WEIGHT 215 lbs (97.5 kg)
EYES Blue-black **HAIR** Black
POWERS The Mandarin's ten rings each produce a different effect—from creating lightning bolts to altering the passage of time. The Mandarin is also a scientific genius and expert martial artist.
ALLIES Fin Fang Foom, Swordsman, Living Laser
FOES Iron Man, Iron Patriot, Squirrel Girl

POWER RINGS
Each of Mandarin's rings has its own unique power. Mandarin wears all ten and has used them to attempt to conquer the Earth.

ENERGY PROJECTION	STRENGTH	DURABILITY	FIGHTING SKILL	INTELLIGENCE	SPEED
6	3	3	6	6	3

POWER RANK

MANIFOLD

Eden Fesi is Manifold, a hero who can open gateways in reality with his hands. He can thus transport heroes across the planet and even to other worlds. He was trained by Gateway, an ally of the X-Men, and recruited by Nick Fury Sr. to work with his Secret Warriors team. Following Gateway's death, Manifold joined the Avengers and helping them to combat the threat of the Titan Thanos and other cosmic foes, moving the Super Heroes where they needed to be in the blink of an eye.

Manifold was being trained by Gateway when Nick Fury got in contact. After Gateway gave his blessing, Manifold decided to help Fury and his Secret Warriors team.

VITAL STATS
REAL NAME Eden Fesi
OCCUPATION Super Hero
BASE Mobile
HEIGHT Unrevealed
WEIGHT Unrevealed
EYES Brown **HAIR** Black
POWERS Fesi tears open holes in reality with his hands, bending it so that he can transport himself and others across vast distances. He is also a skillful hand-to-hand fighter, an expert hunter, and knows how to survive in harsh environments.
ALLIES Avengers, Gateway, Secret Warriors, Nick Fury Sr.
FOES A.I.M., Thanos, Hydra, Baron Strucker

Eden Fesi's portals remain open until he decides to close them.

TRANSPORTER
Manifold's ability to teleport himself and those around him through time and space has proved invaluable to the Avengers.

Eden Fesi is highly skilled with his favorite weapon, a long spear.

	ENERGY PROJECTION	STRENGTH	DURABILITY	FIGHTING SKILL	INTELLIGENCE	SPEED
POWER RANK	3	2	2	4	2	7

MANTIS

Mantis was raised in Vietnam by peaceful alien Kree, guardians of a human-like race of telepathic plants. She trained in martial arts, teaming up with the original Swordsman. The pair fought alongside the Avengers but when Swordsman was killed, Mantis left Earth. She returned to help the Avengers when the Scarlet Witch went crazy. Mantis was also a member of the Guardians of the Galaxy.

Star-Lord convinced Mantis to use her telepathic powers on her fellow heroes so that they would join the modern-day Guardians of the Galaxy.

Mantis' mind is a human/plant hybrid. She is able to communicate with plants telepathically.

VITAL STATS

REAL NAME Unrevealed
OCCUPATION Adventurer
BASE Mobile
HEIGHT 5 ft 6 in (1.67 m)
WEIGHT 115 lbs (52.50 kg)
EYES Green **HAIR** Black
POWERS Mantis has exceptional martial-arts skills. From her contact with alien, sentient plants, she has learned to communicate telepathically with plants. She can also sense the emotions of others.
ALLIES Swordsman (Jacques Duquesne), Silver Surfer, Avengers, Guardians of the Galaxy (modern-day team)
FOES Immortus, Kang, Thanos

GOING GREEN
Mantis once looked human but her skin turned green when she evolved into a powerful being called the Celestial Madonna.

ENERGY PROJECTION	STRENGTH	DURABILITY	FIGHTING SKILL	INTELLIGENCE	SPEED	POWER RANK
3	3	3	6	3	2	

MARIA HILL

Maria Hill took over as director of S.H.I.E.L.D. (Strategic Hazard Intervention, Espionage Logistics Directorate) when Nick Fury had to leave after arranging a secret invasion of Doctor Doom's Latveria. While not popular with many heroes at first, Maria eventually gained their respect when she refused to obey a direct order from the U.S. President to launch a nuclear strike on the island of Genosha, saving the Avengers' lives in the process.

Following Norman Osborn se to power, Maria Hill lost her job as head of S.H.I.E.L.D. She had her revenge though, helping Thor, Iron Man, and other heroes fight Norman Osborn's team during his attempted invasion of Asgard.

VITAL STATS

REAL NAME Maria Hill
OCCUPATION Ex-director of S.H.I.E.L.D.
BASE Mobile
HEIGHT 5 ft 10 in (1.77 m)
WEIGHT 135 lbs (61.25 kg)
EYES Brown
HAIR Black
POWERS She is a trained S.H.I.E.L.D. agent with exceptional leadership skills, and an expert martial artist and markswoman.
ALLIES Dum Dum Dugan, Tony Stark (Iron Man)
FOES Norman Osborn (Iron Patriot), Moonstone

She is an expert in unarmed combat, with fists as deadly as some of her weapons.

Maria has no super-powers, but is very well equipped for battle.

S.H.I.E.L.D. DIRECTOR
Maria Hill had to order the arrest of Captain America at the start of the Super Hero Civil War.

A multitasker, Maria Hill can direct several operations at once.

POWER RANK

ENERGY PROJECTION	STRENGTH	DURABILITY	FIGHTING SKILL	INTELLIGENCE	SPEED
1	2	2	4	4	2

Marrina was one of an alien race called the Plodex. When she turned into a monster during pregnancy, the Avengers tried to stop her. Eventually the Sub-Mariner was forced to kill her, and Marrina has since returned to life to attack him once more.

MARRINA

Fisherman Thomas Smallwood was amazed when a strange egg he found hatched to reveal a green baby girl. Thomas and his wife raised the girl, whom they named Marrina. With a strong affinity for water, she grew up to become a founding member of Canadian Super Hero team Alpha Flight. Marrina married the Sub-Mariner, but when she became pregnant, her alien nature reasserted itself and she turned into a sea monster.

FIRST DATE
When Marrina first met the Sub-Mariner, she showed him her vicious, alien side.

Marrina can take on a humanoid form when humans are around.

Her body is amphibious, with webbed hands and feet, and gills.

VITAL STATS
REAL NAME Marrina Smallwood McKenzie
OCCUPATION Adventurer
BASE Mobile
HEIGHT 6 ft (1.82 m)
WEIGHT 200 lbs (90.75 kg)
EYES Black **HAIR** Green
POWERS Marrina's alien nature makes her able to mimic human and aquatic life. She can live underwater, and at times takes on a bestial state.
ALLIES Namor, the Sub-Mariner, Avengers, Alpha Flight
FOES Master of the World, Norman Osborn (Iron Patriot)

ENERGY PROJECTION	STRENGTH	DURABILITY	FIGHTING SKILL	INTELLIGENCE	SPEED
1	4	3	3	3	4

POWER RANK

MARTINEX

Martinex's ancestors were genetically modified to survive on the harsh world of 31st-century Pluto. After an invasion of the Earth's solar system by the alien Badoon, Martinex joined the Guardians of the Galaxy to fight them. The team also traveled back in time to help the Avengers defeat the cosmic villain Korvac. When Martinex returned to the 31st century he formed the Galactic Guardians, before rejoining the Guardians of the Galaxy.

Martinex left the Guardians of the Galaxy for a while to form the Galactic Guardians. The new team was made up of Martinex, the Spirit of Vengeance, Replica, Phoenix, Firelord, and Hollywood. Their mission was to protect people from alien attack.

VITAL STATS
REAL NAME Martinex T'Naga
OCCUPATION Adventurer, scientist
BASE Mobile
HEIGHT 6 ft 1 in (1.85 m)
WEIGHT 455 lbs (206.5 kg)
EYES Gray
HAIR None
POWERS Martinex is able to withstand extreme temperatures. He can emit blasts of heat from his right hand and cold from his left. With the cold blast, he can also temporarily freeze people.
ALLIES
Guardians of the Galaxy, Avengers
FOES Badoon, Korvac

His right and left hands can generate hot and cold blasts, respectively.

Martinex's powers can only be used for 90 minutes at a time—he must then let them recharge.

ICE COLD
Martinex has the power to freeze people in an alien, ice-like substance without actually killing them.

Martinex's toughened crystal skin enables him to survive in 31st-century Pluto's harsh environment.

POWER RANK

	ENERGY PROJECTION	STRENGTH	DURABILITY	FIGHTING SKILL	INTELLIGENCE	SPEED
	5	3	4	4	4	3

MARVEL BOY

Marvel Boy joined a later incarnation of Young Avengers alongside Hawkeye (Kate Bishop), Power Man, Hulkling, Loki, and Wiccan. He had a brief relationship with Kate Bishop while in the team.

Noh-Varr is a member of the alien Kree from another dimension. He was the only survivor when his starship, *The Marvel*, was shot down by Doctor Midas and crashed on Earth. Noh-Varr, now known as Marvel Boy, was captured by S.H.I.E.L.D. He declared war on humanity, but later events brought about a change of heart. He fought alongside humans during the Skrull Invasion, was part of Norman Osborn's Avengers and later joined the Young Avengers.

He can grow and solidify his hair at will, making it act as a helmet.

Nanotechnology in his saliva causes hallucinations in anyone it touches.

Extra-dense armor is made from alien metal.

Marvel Boy's gauntlet can instantly transform into a gun.

VITAL STATS
REAL NAME Noh-Varr
OCCUPATION Protector of Earth
BASE Mobile
HEIGHT 5 ft 10 in (1.77 m)
WEIGHT 165 lbs (74.75 kg)
EYES Blue **HAIR** White
POWERS Marvel Boy has enhanced strength, extreme speed, super-fast reactions, and super-stamina. He is able to run up walls, possibly due to sheer speed. Nanobots in his bloodstream remove any pain he should feel.
ALLIES Young Avengers, Captain America
FOES Bannermen, Norman Osborn, Mother, Doctor Midas

EARLY MARVELS
Several others have called themselves Marvel Boy, including Wendell Vaughn before he became Quasar.

ENERGY PROJECTION	STRENGTH	DURABILITY	FIGHTING SKILL	INTELLIGENCE	SPEED	POWER RANK
1	4	3	4	4	3	

MASTER PANDEMONIUM

Martin Preston made a deal with the demon Mephisto after losing an arm in a car accident. He became Master Pandemonium—a being of great power, but with a star-shaped hole in his chest that he could only fill by finding the five missing pieces of his soul. In his efforts to find them, he clashed with the West Coast Avengers. He has also attacked Wiccan and Speed of the Young Avengers, believing them to be two of his lost soul fragments.

Master Pandemonium's body contains an army of demons, placed there by Mephisto. His ability to control the demons, known as the Rakasha, makes Master Pandemonium a dangerous enemy.

VITAL STATS

REAL NAME Martin Preston
OCCUPATION
Demon commander
BASE Mobile
HEIGHT 6 ft 1 in (1.85 m)
WEIGHT Unrevealed
EYES Blue (variable)
HAIR Black
POWERS His Amulet of Azmodeus allows interdimensional travel. He can control the army of demons living in his body, and can emit magical fire from his mouth.
ALLIES Rakasha Demons, Mephisto
FOES Scarlet Witch, the Thing, Firebird, Avengers

A star-shaped hole reflects the five missing pieces of his soul.

His arms are two demons, and can be detached from his body.

WEST COAST PANDEMONIUM
Master Pandemonium has clashed with the West Coast Avengers time and again.

POWER RANK	ENERGY PROJECTION	STRENGTH	DURABILITY	FIGHTING SKILL	INTELLIGENCE	SPEED
	7	6	7	3	4	2

MAXIMUS

Maximus is the brother of Black Bolt, the leader of the Inhumans. Power hungry but brilliant, Maximus made several attempts to overthrow his brother and become the Inhumans' ruler, all ending in defeat. The brothers put aside their differences when the Skrulls invaded, Maximus helped the Inhumans defeat them. He later helped Black Bolt to save the Inhumans from Thanos and to spread the Terrigen Mists across the whole world.

Maximus has created weapons and machines that are a threat to everyone. One of the most dangerous was the Omega Construct, a deadly android.

Maximus is able to mentally control those close to him.

TAKEOVER ATTEMPTS
Black Bolt's Inhumans sometimes needed help from the Avengers to oppose his attempts to usurp power.

Maximus' crazed intellect is capable of inventing terrible weapons.

VITAL STATS
REAL NAME Maximus
OCCUPATION Scientist
BASE Attilan
HEIGHT 5 ft 11 in (1.80 m)
WEIGHT 180 lbs (81.75 kg)
EYES Blue **HAIR** Black
POWERS Maximus is a genius inventor, with a superior intellect but hardly any sanity to temper it. He is able to use his thoughts to numb, control, and wipe people's minds, and can even exchange his consciousness with another's.
ALLIES Black Bolt (former enemy)
FOES Skrulls, Fantastic Four, Avengers

ENERGY PROJECTION	STRENGTH	DURABILITY	FIGHTING SKILL	INTELLIGENCE	SPEED	POWER RANK
3	3	3	2	5	3	

M MEDUSA

Medusa is a member of the Inhuman royal family and is married to their leader Black Bolt. At the wedding of her sister Crystal to the Super Hero Quicksilver, Medusa fought alongside the Avengers when Ultron attacked. She has ruled the Inhumans at times when her husband has been missing. Following Attilan's destruction, she started to seek out those humans transformed by the Terrigen Mists to help them come to terms with their new powers.

Medusa and Black Bolt have a closer relationship than most married couples. With a voice capable of causing great devastation, Black Bolt rarely speaks, and relies on Medusa to interpret his wishes to the world.

ROYAL BLOOD
As a member of the Inhuman royal family, Medusa is at the forefront of any conflict.

Her position as the wife of Black Bolt gives her high status among the Inhumans.

Medusa can use her hair as a weapon, a rope, a whip, or even to pick locks.

Her hair is super-strong and she is able to control its growth, shape, and length.

VITAL STATS
REAL NAME Medusa Amaquelin Boltagon
OCCUPATION Queen, royal interpreter
BASE Attilan
HEIGHT 5 ft 11 in (1.80 m)
WEIGHT 130 lbs (59 kg)
EYES Green **HAIR** Red
POWERS Medusa can control her tougher-than-steel hair to the extent that she can control each strand individually. Her power even works if her hair has been cut from her head.
ALLIES Black Bolt, Fantastic Four, Avengers
FOES The Wizard, Trapster, Ultron, Quicksilver

POWER RANK	ENERGY PROJECTION	STRENGTH	DURABILITY	FIGHTING SKILL	INTELLIGENCE	SPEED
	1	3	3	4	3	2

MELTER

Bruno Horgan was an arms dealer until Tony Stark's company put him out of business. As Horgan's company was folding, he found a malfunctioning weapon that could melt anything. Using it as part of a costume, Horgan attacked Stark Industries only to be stopped by Iron Man. He reappeared shortly after as part of the Masters of Evil, taking on the Avengers. Melter was killed by his assistant, who was really an assassin sent by the Scourge.

Melter's ray was powerful enough to melt through Iron Man's armor, making him one of the Avengers' deadlier enemies. Despite attacking Iron Man and his teammates several times, Melter was always eventually defeated.

His high-powered weapon can melt almost anything, from walls to solid steel.

VITAL STATS
REAL NAME Bruno Horgan
OCCUPATION Criminal
BASE Mobile
HEIGHT 6 ft (1.82 m)
WEIGHT 200 lbs (90.75 kg)
EYES Brown **HAIR** Brown
POWERS Horgan's melting device emits a ray that melts objects on a molecular level rather than by using heat. Over the years, Bruno has upgraded his unique weapon to make himself even more deadly.
ALLIES Baron Zemo, Ultron, Doctor Doom
FOES Iron Man, Black Knight, Captain America

YOUNG MASTERS
A new Melter is part of the Young Masters, a Super Villain team who recently fought the Young Avengers.

The Melter has also been known to use guns that can fire deadly melting rays.

ENERGY PROJECTION	STRENGTH	DURABILITY	FIGHTING SKILL	INTELLIGENCE	SPEED	POWER RANK
6	4	5	5	5	4	

METTLE

Ken Mack was an experienced surfer, but when a surfboard struck him in the head, his skin was cut, revealing a tough metallic skin beneath. He turned to Norman Osborn for help. Instead of helping, Osborn experimented on Ken, eventually revealing that under his skin was super-tough flesh made of an iridium-like metal. Ken later joined the Avengers Academy and put on a brave front to mask the isolation he felt in his metallic form.

Mettle's exceptional strength and super-tough body have enabled him to take on dangerous foes such as the mutant Sebastian Shaw.

VITAL STATS
REAL NAME Ken Mack
OCCUPATION Avenger trainee
BASE Avengers Academy
HEIGHT Unrevealed
WEIGHT Unrevealed
EYES Gray **HAIR** None
POWERS Mettle's flesh was transformed into a substance like the metal iridium. It made him exceptionally strong and powerful while also exceptionally durable.
ALLIES Hazmat, Avengers Academy students, Hank Pym, Tigra
FOES Arcade, Jeremy Briggs, Psycho-Man

Mettle's iridium-like flesh made him unable to feel pain or a gentle touch.

SELFLESS SACRIFICE
Mettle had feelings for Avengers student Hazmat, seemingly giving his life to save her from Arcade.

Mettle's metallic condition did not affect his original agility or mobility.

POWER RANK	ENERGY PROJECTION	STRENGTH	DURABILITY	FIGHTING SKILL	INTELLIGENCE	SPEED
	1	5	4	3	2	2

MISS AMERICA

Raised in a utopian reality, Miss America left her home to become a Super Hero, traveling across the dimensions to help others. She came to Earth after meeting the young Loki and, not trusting the Norse God of Mischief, kept a protective eye on Loki's teammates in the Young Avengers. Super-strong with an array of amazing powers, Miss America is a Super Hero with attitude, loyal to her friends and trouble for Super Villains across the Multiverse.

Miss America is especially watchful of Wiccan (in red cloak), who in the future will be the Demiurge—or the main life force—of her home reality.

WORLD WAR II HERO
The first Miss America was Madeline Joyce, a Super Hero who fought alongside the Invaders against the Axis powers during World War II.

Miss America favors normal clothing over a traditional Super Hero costume.

Miss America's skin is bulletproof.

VITAL STATS
REAL NAME America Chavez
OCCUPATION Adventurer
BASE Mobile
HEIGHT Unrevealed
WEIGHT Unrevealed
EYES Brown **HAIR** Black
POWERS Miss America has superhuman strength and durability, and can also fly. She can kick open gateways between dimensions, allowing her to travel easily through different realities.
ALLIES Young Avengers, Runaways, Teen Brigade
FOES Mother (an interdimensional entity), Young Masters of Evil

ENERGY PROJECTION	STRENGTH	DURABILITY	FIGHTING SKILL	INTELLIGENCE	SPEED	POWER RANK
5	5	6	4	3		

MISTER HYDE

Research scientist Calvin Zabo was inspired by Robert Louis Stevenson's story *Dr. Jekyll and Mr. Hyde* to create a potion that worked like the one in the book. The potion brought out his bestial side and also gave him immense strength, and Zabo used it to begin a criminal career as Mister Hyde. He fought the Avengers as part of the Masters of Evil, capturing Jarvis and the Black Knight and nearly killing Hercules before the Avengers stopped him.

The Young Avengers fought Mister Hyde after he was caught selling a version of his dangerous potion. He had told his customers that the potion was MGH (Mutant Growth Hormone), another powerful, but also illegal, drug.

VITAL STATS

REAL NAME Calvin Zabo
OCCUPATION Criminal, former scientist
BASE Mobile
HEIGHT 6 ft 5 in (1.95 m)
WEIGHT 420 lbs (190.5 kg)
EYES Brown **HAIR** Brown
POWERS In his mutated form of Mister Hyde, Zabo has superhuman strength, durability, and resistance to pain. His skin is very tough, providing protection from harm. He switches between his Zabo and Hyde forms by using different versions of the potion.
ALLIES Cobra, Loki, Scorpion, Batroc the Leaper
FOES Avengers, Captain America, Spider-Man, Daredevil

During Zabo's transformations into Mister Hyde, his face wears an evil sneer.

Each transformation takes about 30 seconds, and is very painful.

DARING ESCAPE
When breaking out of the Raft prison, Mister Hyde met his nemesis, Daredevil.

POWER RANK	ENERGY PROJECTION	STRENGTH	DURABILITY	FIGHTING SKILL	INTELLIGENCE	SPEED
	1	6	3	4	5	2

MISTER IMMORTAL

When Craig Hollis was a young boy, his mother asked Deathurge to watch over him. From that point on, no matter how reckless Craig was, he couldn't die. Each time he was killed, he kept coming back to life with any injuries he had suffered fully healed. He decided to use his power for the greater good and, as Mister Immortal, formed the Great Lakes Avengers. He has recently learned that it is his destiny to outlive everyone else in the world in order to learn one last great secret.

Although Craig Hollis has died many times, he always recovers instantly. He has survived many deaths, including being burned, drowned, blown up, poisoned, and decapitated.

Mister Immortal wears sunglasses as a tribute to the X-Men's Cyclops.

Mister Immortal likes to change his look and has gone through several costume changes.

VITAL STATS
REAL NAME Craig Hollis
OCCUPATION Adventurer
BASE Great Lakes
HEIGHT 6 ft 2 in (1.88 m)
WEIGHT 156 lbs (70.75 kg)
EYES Blue
HAIR Blond
POWERS Mister Immortal cannot permanently die. Each time he is killed, he swiftly revives, fully healed. He also seems to have stopped aging.
ALLIES Great Lakes Avengers, Deathurge, Deadpool
FOES Maelstrom, Graviton, Batroc

ODDBALL HEROES
The Great Lakes Avengers was a bizarre-looking team with powers to match.

ENERGY PROJECTION	STRENGTH	DURABILITY	FIGHTING SKILL	INTELLIGENCE	SPEED
1	2	7	2	4	2

POWER RANK

125

MOCKINGBIRD

Bobbi Morse is an ex-S.H.I.E.L.D. agent who took the name of Mockingbird. She joined the Avengers shortly after meeting Hawkeye (Clint Barton), with whom she became romantically involved. The two went on to form the West Coast Avengers together. Mockingbird left the team for a while, but returned to help mentor the Great Lakes Avengers. She was thought to have died while saving Hawkeye from an attack by Mephisto, but was later revealed to be held as a prisoner of the Skrulls.

A spell in Skrull captivity did nothing to dampen Mockingbird's taste for danger. Since her release, she has returned to adventuring with Hawkeye.

VITAL STATS

REAL NAME Barbara "Bobbi" Morse
OCCUPATION Adventurer
BASE Mobile
HEIGHT 5 ft 9 in (1.75 m)
WEIGHT 135 lbs (61.25 kg)
EYES Blue **HAIR** Blonde
POWERS Mockingbird has no super-powers but is an expert fighter with full S.H.I.E.L.D. training. She is extremely tough and combative.
ALLIES Hawkeye, Captain America, Ka-Zar, Great Lakes Avengers
FOES Crossfire, Phantom Rider

Her costume is made of Kevlar and Beta cloth, and is bulletproof and fire resistant.

Mockingbird holds a doctoral degree in biology.

LOVE AND WAR
Mockingbird married Clint Barton (Hawkeye) and fought with him in the West Coast Avengers.

Her two staves can be used as clubs or joined to form a battle staff.

POWER RANK	ENERGY PROJECTION	STRENGTH	DURABILITY	FIGHTING SKILL	INTELLIGENCE	SPEED
	1	2	2	6	3	

M.O.D.O.K.

M.O.D.O.K. has been a longtime enemy of Captain America. Along with his A.I.M. agents, M.O.D.O.K. has had numerous masterplans disrupted by Cap and his allies.

M.O.D.O.K. Stands for Mobile Organism Designed Only for Killing. He was once A.I.M. agent George Tarleton, chosen by A.I.M. to become a humanoid supercomputer. The experiment mutated George and drove him insane. Originally called M.O.D.O.C., with the last letter standing for "Computing," George decided the last letter should be a K, for "Killing." Since becoming A.I.M.'s leader, he has terrorized the world. He also has his own gang, M.O.D.O.K.'s 11.

M.O.D.O.K.'S NEMESIS
Captain Marvel Carol Danvers is a longtime enemy of M.O.D.O.K. She has defeated him numerous times.

M.O.D.O.K.'s headband is a teleportation device.

M.O.D.O.K. wears powered armor over his feeble limbs.

M.O.D.O.K. is unable to move without his hoverchair.

VITAL STATS
REAL NAME George Tarleton
OCCUPATION Terrorist
BASE Unknown
HEIGHT 12 ft (3.66 m)
WEIGHT 750 lbs (340.19 kg)
EYES White **HAIR** Black
POWERS M.O.D.O.K. has superhuman mental and telepathic powers and a computer-like brain. His hoverchair allows him to fly and is armed with various weapons. He can also teleport.
ALLIES M.O.D.O.K.'s 11 (a gang of hired villains), Intelligencia (a group of criminal masterminds)
FOES Captain Marvel (Carol Danvers), Captain America, Iron Man, Avengers

ENERGY PROJECTION	STRENGTH	DURABILITY	FIGHTING SKILL	INTELLIGENCE	SPEED	POWER RANK
6	5	5	1	6		

MONICA CHANG

Monica Chang is the head of S.H.I.E.L.D.'s artificial intelligence division. A computer expert and fully trained agent with exceptional leadership skills, she was given the job of interrogating scientist Hank Pym when a computer virus that he had created to destroy the evil robot Ultron gained sentience and became a threat. Working with Pym she became part of the Avengers A.I. team, helping to protect the world from threats posed by Artificial Intelligence.

Monica Chang was one of the first people to join Avengers A.I., the team brought together to help combat attacks linked to artificial intelligence. Her S.H.I.E.L.D. status proved invaluable for the team.

VITAL STATS

REAL NAME Monica Chang
OCCUPATION Chief of S.H.I.E.L.D.'s Artificial Intelligence Division
BASE Mobile
HEIGHT Unrevealed
WEIGHT Unrevealed
EYES Black **HAIR** Black
POWERS Monica is a fully trained S.H.I.E.L.D. agent with exceptional fighting and combat skills. She is also a computer expert.
ALLIES Hank Pym, Avengers, Nick Fury
FOES Dimitrios

Monica is skilled with various high-tech weapons.

TOUGH TALK
Monica Chang met Hank Pym when she had to question him about the defeat of Ultron and to find out his connection to newly created A.I. threat Dimitrios. With the danger level severe, she didn't pull her punches.

Monica wears a standard-issue S.H.I.E.L.D. uniform.

POWER RANK	ENERGY PROJECTION	STRENGTH	DURABILITY	FIGHTING SKILL	INTELLIGENCE	SPEED
	1	2	2	4	3	2

While Moon Knight prefers to work alone, he has sometimes teamed up with other vigilantes such as the Punisher and Spider-Man.

MOON KNIGHT

Marc Spector was a mercenary left for dead in the Egyptian desert. He was saved by followers of the Egyptian God Khonshu, who gave him superhuman powers. On his return to the U.S.A., he began to carry out Khonshu's will by punishing criminals. As Moon Knight, he later joined the West Coast Avengers, learning that some of his equipment had been created in ancient Egypt by a time-traveling Hawkeye (Clint Barton).

His cape can also be used as a glider.

AMAZING AIRCRAFT
Moon Knight has had various highly advanced aircraft, including the Mooncopter and Angelwing.

The crescent moon is a symbol of Khonshu, the Egyptian god.

VITAL STATS
REAL NAME Marc Spector
OCCUPATION Millionaire playboy, vigilante
BASE New York City
HEIGHT 6 ft 2 in (1.87 m)
WEIGHT 225 lbs (102 kg)
EYES Dark Brown **HAIR** Brown
POWERS Moon Knight's strength increases and decreases as the moon waxes and wanes. He has an arsenal of weaponry given to him by the Egyptian God Khonshu.
ALLIES Spider-Man, Tigra, Frenchie, Marlene Alraune, Punisher
FOES Black Spectre, Bushman, Midnight Man

ENERGY PROJECTION	STRENGTH	DURABILITY	FIGHTING SKILL	INTELLIGENCE	SPEED	POWER RANK
1	3	3	4	2	2	

MOONDRAGON

Moondragon was born on Earth, but after Thanos killed her parents, she was taken to Saturn's moon Titan and raised by the monks of Shao-Lom. They taught her martial arts and helped her to develop psionic powers. Returning to Earth, she fought alongside the Avengers and helped the team defeat Korvac. She later learned that her father was alive and had become Drax. She also fought alongside the Guardians of the Galaxy.

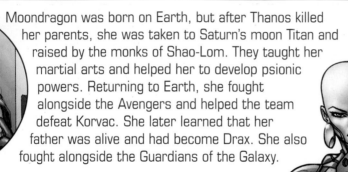

Moondragon helped Rick Jones, Genis-Vell, and their allies when the former Captain Marvel started to go insane due to his cosmic awareness.

MIND ATTACKS
Moondragon can launch powerful psychic attacks on her enemies which makes her a formidable foe.

Moondragon sometimes wears lightweight body armor on missions.

She has total control of her body due to years of practicing Shao-Lom martial arts.

Moondragon is a powerful telekinetic telepath and can use her powers to levitate and fly.

VITAL STATS

REAL NAME Heather Douglas
OCCUPATION Adventurer
BASE Mobile
HEIGHT 6 ft 3 in (1.90 m)
WEIGHT 150 lbs (68 kg)
EYES Blue
HAIR None
POWERS Moondragon is a highly trained martial artist. She is also a powerful telepath, able to control minds, alter personalities, and modify memories. Her telekinetic powers give her control over physical objects and enable her to fire mental blasts at enemies.
ALLIES Phyla-Vell, Defenders, Avengers
FOES Ultron, Thanos, Korvac

POWER RANK

ENERGY PROJECTION	STRENGTH	DURABILITY	FIGHTING SKILL	INTELLIGENCE	SPEED
5	3	3	4	4	3

MOONSTONE

Moonstone took on the role of Ms. Marvel as part of Norman Osborn's Avengers line-up, defeating the real Ms. Marvel in the process.

Doctor Karla Sofen is a psychologist who took a Kree lifestone from the original Moonstone, Lloyd Bloch, to gain super-powers. She used her powers for her own ends and soon became a notorious Super Villain, fighting alongside the Masters of Evil before joining the Thunderbolts. Moonstone was also part of Luke Cage's new line-up of the Thunderbolts.

Moonstone is a master manipulator and often uses people to further her own ends.

Moonstone can emit laser beams from her hands.

The Kree lifestone gives Karla the power to alter her costume at will.

VITAL STATS
REAL NAME Karla Sofen
OCCUPATION Psychologist
BASE Thunderbolts Mountain
HEIGHT 5 ft 11 in (1.80 m)
WEIGHT 130 lbs (59 kg)
EYES Blue **HAIR** Blonde
POWERS Using the power of the moonstone—part of a Kree lifestone—Karla is able to fly, become intangible, and emit blinding bursts of light. Additional moonstones increase and diversify her powers.
ALLIES Baron Zemo, Norman Osborn (Iron Patriot), Thunderbolts
FOES Marvel Boy, Ms. Marvel, Avengers

LIGHTNING JUSTICE
Moonstone joined the original line-up of the Thunderbolts as Meteorite to conceal her identity.

ENERGY PROJECTION	STRENGTH	DURABILITY	FIGHTING SKILL	INTELLIGENCE	SPEED
4	4	3	3	4	3

POWER RANK

MORDRED

Mordred the Evil was the treacherous son of King Arthur and was instrumental in bringing about the fall of Camelot. His rival was Sir Percy, the Black Knight, who managed to overthrow many of his wicked schemes. The two finally killed each other in combat, but Mordred was resurrected by his aunt, the sorceress Morgan Le Fay. Mordred and Morgan have since joined forces several times against the Avengers.

Mordred fought alongside Morgan Le Fay when she used the Scarlet Witch's powers to remake reality into her own mythical dominion.

VITAL STATS
REAL NAME Sir Mordred
OCCUPATION Knight, conqueror
BASE Mobile
HEIGHT 5 ft 10 in (1.77 m)
WEIGHT 185 lbs (84 kg)
EYES Blue
HAIR Black
POWERS Mordred is a powerful swordsman whose natural skills and strength have been heightened by Morgan Le Fay. He is also an expert horseman and jouster, skills developed during his life at King Arthur's court in Camelot.
ALLIES Morgan Le Fay
FOES Captain Britain, the Black Knight, Lionheart, Avengers

Born in the days of Camelot, he is kept in peak condition by Morgan Le Fay's sorcery.

Mordred is one of the most despised villains in history.

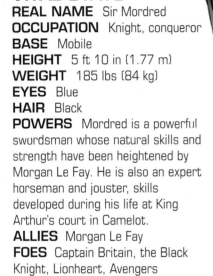

LONDON CALLING
Mordred once helped his mother attempt to destroy London.

POWER RANK	ENERGY PROJECTION	STRENGTH	DURABILITY	FIGHTING SKILL	INTELLIGENCE	SPEED
	6	2	7	5	3	2

MORGAN LE FAY

Morgan Le Fay is the half-sister of King Arthur and one of the most powerful magicians of all time. A troublemaker, she has plotted against King Arthur and been imprisoned by Merlin. Over the years Morgan has fought the Avengers more than once. She recently traveled forward in time to the present to take revenge on Doctor Doom, who had betrayed her trust. She was defeated and sent back to prehistoric times.

Morgan Le Fay once ruled a mythical realm where the Avengers fought as her guards. They eventually broke free and returned reality to normal.

Morgan's powers reach beyond time and space.

EVIL PAST AND PRESENT
Norman Osborn's Avengers fought with the sorceress when she traveled to the present to kill Doctor Doom.

Morgan Le Fay uses powerful magic to keep herself young and beautiful.

VITAL STATS
REAL NAME Morgan Le Fay
OCCUPATION Sorceress
BASE Astral Plane
HEIGHT 6 ft 2 in (1.87 m)
WEIGHT 140 lbs (63.50 kg)
EYES Green **HAIR** Black
POWERS Half faerie, Morgan is a powerful sorceress and shape changer. She can summon and control magical creatures and manipulate others with her mind. She is also able to project energy, travel across time, space, and dimensions, and fly.
ALLIES Mordred the Evil
FOES Doctor Doom, Avengers, Captain Britain

ENERGY PROJECTION	STRENGTH	DURABILITY	FIGHTING SKILL	INTELLIGENCE	SPEED
6	2	6	2	4	2

POWER RANK

MS. MARVEL

Kamala Khan was a normal teenager until she found herself enveloped in the Terrigen mists (unleashed on the world by Black Bolt). The mists gave Kamala shape-changing abilities. At first, Kamala took on the appearance of her hero, Captain Marvel (Carol Danvers). However, she soon developed her own identity and costume as the latest Ms. Marvel. She's now the protector of New Jersey, sneaking out at night to fight crime—as long as her parents don't ground her!

The first few times Kamala used her shape-changing powers, she found herself transformed into the Carol Danvers' version of Ms. Marvel. She was even shot while Ms. Marvel—but her new powers saved her.

VITAL STATS

REAL NAME Kamala Khan
OCCUPATION Super Hero
BASE New Jersey
HEIGHT 5 ft 4 in (1.63 m)
WEIGHT Unrevealed
EYES Brown **HAIR** Brown
POWERS Kamala is a polymorph and can increase or decrease the size and shape of her body or part of her body at will. She also has healing abilities and has survived a gunshot from point-blank range. She can also transform to take on the appearance of other people.
ALLIES Captain America, Wolverine, Lockjaw
FOES Inventor

Ms. Marvel's mask conceals her heroic identity from her parents.

The lightning bolt is a tribute to the previous Ms. Marvel.

RAPID RESPONSE
At first Kamala had little control over her powers but she rapidly gained in confidence and skill.

POWER RANK	ENERGY PROJECTION	STRENGTH	DURABILITY	FIGHTING SKILL	INTELLIGENCE	SPEED
	1	4	4	2	3	3

MVP

College sports star Michael Van Patrick was the great-grandson of Doctor Abraham Erskine, creator of the Super Soldier Serum that gave Captain America his powers. When Van Patrick's family history was made public he was kicked out of college, despite there being no evidence of performance-enhancing substances in his blood. He was recruited to the Avengers Initiative training program, where he adopted the codename MVP. Unfortunately he was killed in his first training session.

It was discovered that MVP had naturally perfect DNA, and it was later used to create several clones. Three of the clones became new Scarlet Spiders named Michael, Van, and Patrick. All but one of these clones died.

After MVP's death, Initiative scientist, Baron Von Blitzschlag, kept his body in order to study it further.

CRAZY CLONE
One of MVP's clones went insane. Calling itself KIA, it went on a killing spree and attacked the Initiative.

Many people believed that MVP's skills were a result of exposure to his great-grandfather's Super Soldier Serum.

VITAL STATS
REAL NAME Michael Van Patrick
OCCUPATION Adventurer
BASE Camp Hammond
HEIGHT 5 ft 11 in (1.80 m)
WEIGHT 173 lbs (78.5 kg)
EYES Blue **HAIR** Brown
POWERS MVP was at the peak of physical perfection, possessing exceptional speed, strength, stamina, and reflexes.
ALLIES Cloud 9, Trauma, Hardball, Komodo, Thor Girl, Gauntlet
FOES Baron Von Blitzschlag, Henry Peter Gyrich

ENERGY PROJECTION	STRENGTH	DURABILITY	FIGHTING SKILL	INTELLIGENCE	SPEED	POWER RANK
1	2	2	3	2	2	

NEBULA

Nebula is a powerful enemy of the Avengers. She has claimed to be the granddaughter of Thanos, one of the Eternals, but Thanos denies this. Nebula used his old flagship, *Sanctuary II*, to become a space pirate and sought to take over the Skrull Empire, but the Avengers stopped her. She came close to wresting the Infinity Gauntlet from Thanos and has also fought as one of the Graces, a team of female warriors created by Gamora.

Nebula and Thanos came into conflict when both sought the powerful Infinity Gauntlet. At one point Nebula came close to destroying Thanos, before losing her cosmic power.

VITAL STATS

REAL NAME Unrevealed
OCCUPATION Pirate, mercenary
BASE Mobile
HEIGHT 6 ft 1 in (1.85 m)
WEIGHT 185 lbs (84 kg)
EYES Blue **HAIR** Black
POWERS Nebula is an excellent strategist, marksman, and leader. She is armed with various high-tech weapons such as wrist-mounted energy blasters. She can lift up to 60 tons (54.43 tonnes) and her chameleon outfit allows her to alter her appearance at will.
ALLIES Skurge, Levan, Gamora
FOES Photon, Avengers, Thanos

Nebula possesses many high-tech gadgets and weapons of alien origin.

A cyborg, Nebula has an artificial left arm, shoulder, and eye.

Nebula has blue skin due to her origins on the planet Luphom.

INFINITY AND BEYOND
The Infinity Gauntlet gave Nebula the power to reshape all existence—power that proved too much for her mind to bear.

POWER RANK

ENERGY PROJECTION	STRENGTH	DURABILITY	FIGHTING SKILL	INTELLIGENCE	SPEED
6	5	3	4	4	2

NICK FURY

Marcus Johnson was an Army Ranger when he learned he was the son of superspy Nick Fury Sr. One of his father's enemies, Orion, wanted the Infinity Formula running through Marcus and his father's body to restore his own youth. Marcus and Nick stopped Orion, but Marcus lost an eye—the villain wanting to make him look more like his father. Marcus adopted his birth name of Nick Fury and joined the security agency S.H.I.E.L.D.

Nick Fury Sr. was a World War II veteran whose life was extended by the Infinity Formula. He went on to become Director of S.H.I.E.L.D. while also secretly protecting Earth from alien attacks.

Nick Fury lost his left eye while battling the Super Villain Orion.

VITAL STATS

REAL NAME Nicholas Fury (previously Marcus Johnson)
OCCUPATION Spy
BASE Mobile
HEIGHT Unrevealed
WEIGHT Unrevealed
EYES Brown **HAIR** Bald
POWERS Nick Fury's aging has been slowed due to the Infinity Formula he inherited from his father. He is a trained Army Ranger, able to survive in the toughest of surroundings. He is also an excellent strategist and trained in the use of various weapons and fighting styles.
ALLIES Avengers, Phillip Coulson, Wolverine, Nick Fury Sr.
FOES Orion, Taskmaster

Nick's S.H.I.E.L.D. uniform provides some protection from shrapnel and other forms of projectile attack.

SECRET AVENGER
Fury created the Secret Avengers team to take on covert missions.

ENERGY PROJECTION	STRENGTH	DURABILITY	FIGHTING SKILL	INTELLIGENCE	SPEED	POWER RANK
1	2	2	6	3	2	

NIGHTMASK

An artificial human created by Ex Nihilo on Mars, Nightmask also goes by the name of Adam. He was brought back to Earth by the Avengers. At first the only language he could speak belonged to the mysterious "Builders," the cosmic race behind Ex Nihilo and his kin. Captain Universe gave Nightmask the ability to speak human languages. He quickly became a key member of the Avengers fighting foes such as Thanos, A.I.M., and Morgan Le Fay.

Tony Stark at first thought Adam's name was Blackveil. Captain Universe appeared and explained that this was a mistranslation and he was actually called Nightmask.

VITAL STATS
REAL NAME Adam
OCCUPATION Super Hero
BASE Avengers Tower, N.Y.C.
HEIGHT Unrevealed
WEIGHT Unrevealed
EYES Pink **HAIR** None
POWERS Nightmask can control and alter machinery. He can also discharge energy in a variety of forms, including powerful blasts. He can create portals to teleport anywhere he can think of, including from Earth to Mars.
ALLIES Avengers, Captain Universe, Ex Nihilo
FOES A.I.M., Thanos, Morgan Le Fay

Nightmask's powers create light-blue energy halos around his body when in use.

Adam is a living being, made by Ex Nihilo in the image of a human.

BATTLING THE UNDEAD
Nightmask was part of the Avengers team that took on the undead hordes of Morgan Le Fay.

POWER RANK	ENERGY PROJECTION	STRENGTH	DURABILITY	FIGHTING SKILL	INTELLIGENCE	SPEED
	6	2	2	1	5	7

NIKKI

Nicholette "Nikki" Gold's ancestors had been genetically altered to survive on 31st-century Mercury. She joined the Guardians of the Galaxy after they discovered her on an abandoned spaceship, apparently the only survivor of her colony. During her time with the Guardians of the Galaxy she had a relationship with Charlie-27, but the two parted. Nikki once traveled back to the present where she fought alongside Spider-Man against the villainous pair Hammer and Anvil.

After traveling back in time with the Guardians of the Galaxy to stop Korvac, Nikki and her teammates nearly became members of the Avengers. In the end, they decided to return to their own time.

Nikki's orange and red hair is styled to resemble flames.

ALIEN CONTROL
In the future world of the Guardians of the Galaxy, the Badoon have conquered the human race.

She changes her costume as often as possible.

Following clashes with the Badoon, Nikki has a particular dislike for reptilian races, such as the Badoon, Skrulls, and Snarks.

VITAL STATS
REAL NAME Nicholette "Nikki" Gold
OCCUPATION Adventurer
BASE Mobile
HEIGHT 5 ft 8 in (1.72 m)
WEIGHT 130 lbs (59 kg)
EYES Red **HAIR** Orange, tinted with red and yellow
POWERS Nikki is a talented acrobat and sharpshooter, and can survive the hot climate of Mercury.
ALLIES Spider-Man, Avengers, Guardians of the Galaxy
FOES Korvac, Hammer and Anvil, Badoon

ENERGY PROJECTION	STRENGTH	DURABILITY	FIGHTING SKILL	INTELLIGENCE	SPEED	POWER RANK
3	3	4	4	2	4	

NORMAN OSBORN

Whether as the crazed Super Villain Green Goblin, the powerful Iron Patriot (with armor stolen from Tony Stark) or as Mason Banks, head of the Alchemax chemical corporation, Norman Osborn is constantly plotting new ways to achieve power. He invented the Goblin Formula, which gave him super-powers but also drove him insane. As the Green Goblin, Osborn has proved to be Spider-Man's archenemy and he remains a menace to heroes everywhere.

Following Osborn's fall from grace as head of H.A.M.M.E.R. (his evil alternative to S.H.I.E.L.D.), he altered his body using A.I.M. technology to give himself the powers of the Super-Adaptoid.

VITAL STATS
REAL NAME Norman Osborn
OCCUPATION Businessman, criminal, Super Villain
BASE Mobile
HEIGHT 5 ft 11 in (1.80 m)
WEIGHT 185 lbs (84 kg)
EYES Blue **HAIR** Reddish brown
POWERS The Green Goblin Formula gave Osborn superhuman strength, reactions, and regenerative abilities. It also caused insanity. With the Super-Adaptoid's powers, Osborn could copy any power belonging to the original Avengers.
ALLIES H.A.M.M.E.R., Moonstone
FOES Spider-Man, Iron Man, Captain America, Avengers, Skaar

Norman Osborn is obsessed with obtaining power for himself.

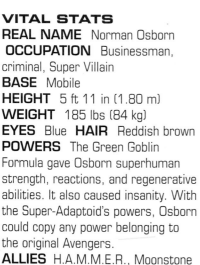

GOBLIN KING
Osborn plotted Spider-Man's destruction, taking on the persona of crime lord the Goblin King.

POWER RANK	ENERGY PROJECTION	STRENGTH	DURABILITY	FIGHTING SKILL	INTELLIGENCE	SPEED
	3	4	4	3	4	3

NOVA

Teenager Sam Alexander is the latest human to become Nova, a cosmic hero linked to the Nova Corps, an intergalactic peacekeeping force. Sam's father was a member of the Corps but vanished in mysterious circumstances. When Gamora and Rocket Raccoon gave Sam his father's helmet, he was transformed into the new Nova. Sam had no knowledge of Nova's past and is still learning to use his abilities.

An earlier incarnation of Nova was Richard Rider. The hero fought alongside Star-Lord and other heroes to save the universe from the schemes of the mad Titan Thanos.

Nova's helmet gives him access to the Nova force, the source of his super-powers.

Nova's costume enables him to function in the vacuum of space.

VITAL STATS
REAL NAME Sam Alexander
OCCUPATION Student
BASE Carefree, Arizona
HEIGHT Unrevealed
WEIGHT Unrevealed
EYES Blue **HAIR** Black
POWERS Access to the Nova force gives Sam superhuman strength, speed, the ability to travel through space, energy projection, and the ability to understand and converse in all languages.
ALLIES Avengers, Beta Ray Bill, Spider-Man, New Warriors, Guardians of the Galaxy
FOES Terrax, Diamondhead, Thanos

HERO WORSHIP
Sam is still awestruck when he meets many of Earth's Super Heroes—especially members of the Avengers.

ENERGY PROJECTION	STRENGTH	DURABILITY	FIGHTING SKILL	INTELLIGENCE	SPEED	POWER RANK
6	7	7	3	2		

PAGAN

Pagan and his brother, Lord Templar, died as children but were resurrected by Jonathan Tremont, a third brother, using a shard of mystic light. Pagan was now endowed with super-powers and began to work for Tremont, whose organization, the Triune, existed solely to increase his own power. After being sent to battle the Avengers, Pagan had his life-force drained shortly before Tremont was defeated by the Avengers and Triathlon, who became the new 3-D Man.

Pagan's strength seemed to increase the wilder he became—and it was not difficult to make him wild. Usually existing in a state of barely suppressed rage, he became almost uncontrollable when riled up for battle.

VITAL STATS

REAL NAME Unknown
OCCUPATION Agent of Jonathan Tremont
BASE Mobile
HEIGHT Unrevealed
WEIGHT Unrevealed
EYES Red **HAIR** Black
POWERS Possessing superhuman strength and durability, Pagan was able to withstand superhuman punches and magical hexes. The angrier he became, the greater his strength.
ALLIES Jonathan Tremont, Lord Templar
FOES Avengers

BROTHERS IN ARMS
Pagan's resurrected brother, Lord Templar, fought alongside him in Tremont's service.

Pagan's strength could grow to unimaginable levels when he became mad.

POWER RANK	ENERGY PROJECTION	STRENGTH	DURABILITY	FIGHTING SKILL	INTELLIGENCE	SPEED
	6	6	6	6	5	6

PHILLIP COULSON

As an agent of S.H.I.E.L.D., Coulson helped to bring together a new group of "Secret" Avengers to attack subversive threats to world security, such as A.I.M.

Phil Coulson fought alongside Marcus Johnson in the Army Rangers and helped his friend to discover that he was the son of famous spymaster Nick Fury Sr. When Marcus—now also calling himself Nick Fury—joined S.H.I.E.L.D., so did Coulson. He was brought into a covert team of heroes known as the Secret Avengers by Maria Hill. As part of the team, Coulson has fought the cybernetic killing machine known as the Fury and worked alongside M.O.D.O.K.

He prefers to wear a suit to help him blend in with the crowd.

Coulson is highly trained with various weapons.

VITAL STATS
REAL NAME Phillip Coulson
OCCUPATION S.H.I.E.L.D. agent
BASE Mobile
HEIGHT 6 ft (1.83 m)
WEIGHT 203 lbs (92 kg)
EYES Blue **HAIR** Brown
POWERS Coulson's light-hearted charm conceals one of S.H.I.E.L.D.'s best agents. He is an Army Ranger with extensive combat experience, a weapons expert, and trained in unarmed combat and espionage techniques. He also has exceptional leadership skills.
ALLIES Nick Fury, Maria Hill, Hawkeye, Avengers
FOES Orion, the Fury, A.I.M.

PHIL'S NICKNAME
Coulson was nicknamed "Cheese" while fighting alongside his friend, the future Nick Fury, as an Army Ranger.

ENERGY PROJECTION	STRENGTH	DURABILITY	FIGHTING SKILL	INTELLIGENCE	SPEED	**POWER RANK**
1	2	2	3	3	2	

PHOBOS

Alex is the son of Ares, the Olympian god of war and an unknown mortal woman. He was raised in secret by Ares, leading a normal life in New Jersey until he discovered that he was the son of a god. The young Alex was kidnapped by the evil Amatsu-Mikaboshi and brainwashed into attacking his father. Zeus, king of the Olympian gods, freed Alex from Mikaboshi's control. Alex later joined the New Warriors as Phobos, having learned he was the Olympian god of fear reborn.

The young Phobos became part of the Secret Warriors. His teammates included Druid, Slingshot, Daisy Johnson, Hellfire, and Stonewall.

VITAL STATS

REAL NAME Alexander Aaron
OCCUPATION God of fear
BASE Olympus
HEIGHT 5 ft 1 in (1.55 m)
WEIGHT 95 lbs (44 kg)
EYES Blue **HAIR** Blond
POWERS Alex can instill fear into others just by looking into their eyes. He can also catch glimpses of the future. As he matures, his powers will increase.
ALLIES Ares, Secret Warriors, Zeus
FOES Gorgon, Hydra, Skrulls, Baron Strucker

When using his fear-instilling powers, Alex's eyes glow.

GOD OF WAR
Alex's father is Ares, the Olympian god of war. When Alex's mortal body was killed by Gorgon, he was reunited with his father in Elysium.

Belt contains normal Secret Warriors field equipment.

POWER RANK

ENERGY PROJECTION	STRENGTH	DURABILITY	FIGHTING SKILL	INTELLIGENCE	SPEED
3	2	2	3	2	2

POWER MAN

While the young Victor considers Luke Cage one of his heroes, the two have also had the odd tussle, Victor's *chi* power proving more than a match for Luke's raw strength.

Victor Alvarez is the son of the Super Villain Shades, an old enemy of Luke Cage (the original Power Man). Shades was killed when their old tenement building was destroyed in a Super Hero battle. His energy-projecting visor shattered in the destruction and fragments were embedded in Victor's body, giving him the ability to absorb life force or *chi*. As Power Man, Victor was trained by Iron Fist, before joining Luke Cage's Mighty Avengers team.

A POWERFUL TEAM-UP
Victor formed a team with Danny Rand, Iron Fist, who helped the young hero train and control his abilities.

Power Man's body glows when he collects *chi*.

Power Man can direct his *chi* energy through his muscles, increasing his punching power.

VITAL STATS
REAL NAME Victor Herman Alvarez
OCCUPATION Adventurer, student, Rand Foundation employee
BASE New York
HEIGHT 5 ft 9 in (1.75 m)
WEIGHT 160 lbs (72.5 kg)
EYES Brown **HAIR** Black
POWERS Victor absorbs *chi* from his environment to gain superhuman strength and accelerated healing. He can direct his *chi* through punches and kicks and also use it to improve the health or enhance the powers of others.
ALLIES Luke Cage, Iron Fist, Avengers Academy students, Mighty Avengers, Amadeus Cho
FOES The Serpent, The Worthy, Proxima Midnight, Shuma-Gorath

ENERGY PROJECTION	STRENGTH	DURABILITY	FIGHTING SKILL	INTELLIGENCE	SPEED	POWER RANK
3	5	5	5	2	2	

PROCTOR

Proctor was an evil version of the Black Knight from a parallel world. On Proctor's Earth, he became the Gann Josin (lifemate) of the Eternal Sersi, but their relationship ended badly when the unstable Sersi turned on her fellow Avengers. She destroyed the world, rejecting Proctor as she did so. In revenge, Proctor formed the Gatherers and traveled across the dimensions, killing Sersi and any allies she had in a multitude of parallel versions of Earth.

Proctor and the Black Knight had several ferocious battles as the villain sought to continue his destructive rampage across the multiverse. While the Black Knight eventually defeated Proctor, he was forced to flee Earth.

VITAL STATS

REAL NAME Unrevealed

OCCUPATION Leader of the Gatherers

BASE Mobile

HEIGHT 6 ft (1.82 m)

WEIGHT 190 lbs (62.5 kg)

EYES Red, with no pupils

HAIR Black

POWERS He has superhuman strength, speed, stamina, and reflexes. His powers are aided by advanced alien technology.

ALLIES Sersi (of a parallel world), evil versions of various Avengers from other worlds

FOES Black Knight, Sersi, Vision, Avengers

Proctor's glowing red eyes are the result of becoming a Gann Josin.

His armor and sword use advanced technology of an unspecified nature.

THE GATHERERS
Proctor was accompanied by the Gatherers, a group made up of evil versions of the Avengers.

POWER RANK	ENERGY PROJECTION	STRENGTH	DURABILITY	FIGHTING SKILL	INTELLIGENCE	SPEED
	5	4	4	4	3	3

PSYKLOP

Psyklop was part of an insect race that once ruled the world. After displeasing the Dark Gods they worshipped they were put into hibernation, but Psyklop was reawakened by the Dark Gods and ordered to find a power source. He tried to use the Hulk's energy but was stopped by the Avengers. Psyklop pursued the Hulk, whom he had shrunk to microscopic size, to the sub-atomic world of K'ai. Psyklop eventually died there.

Psyklop used his advanced technology to shrink the Hulk down to sub-atomic scale, but was interrupted by the Avengers while doing so. While Psyklop was fighting them, the Hulk vanished—reappearing on K'ai.

Psyklop's single eye could hypnotize people and fire energy beams.

Psyklop used alien technology to shrink himself to sub-atomic size.

Psyklop's alien costume expanded or shrank when he changed size.

VITAL STATS
REAL NAME Psyklop
OCCUPATION Servant of the Dark Gods
BASE Mobile
HEIGHT 8 ft (2.43 m), but was variable
WEIGHT 450 lbs (204 kg), but was variable
EYES Red **HAIR** None
POWERS Psyklop possessed exceptional strength and speed. His eye blasts emitted hypnotic power, enabling him to force others to do his will or make them see a distorted reality.
ALLIES Dark Gods
FOES Hulk, Avengers, Jarella

HULK IN PERIL
On the planet K'ai, the Hulk faced countless dangers before Psyklop caught up with him.

ENERGY PROJECTION	STRENGTH	DURABILITY	FIGHTING SKILL	INTELLIGENCE	SPEED
3	5	3	3	5	

POWER RANK

PURPLE MAN

While on a mission, spy Zebediah Killgrave found himself covered from head to foot in an experimental liquid nerve gas. His skin turned purple and he gained the ability to control others. Killgrave began calling himself the Purple Man and embarked on a life of crime. He used his new powers to force others to do his will, including Jessica Jones and the Super Hero Daredevil. He eventually started to run a Las Vegas casino while trying to establish a criminal empire.

The Purple Man joined forces with Avalanche, Headhunter, Shocker, Death Stalker, and a new incarnation of Scourge to start a new criminal cartel with himself as boss.

VITAL STATS
REAL NAME Zebediah Killgrave
OCCUPATION Casino manager, crime boss
BASE Las Vegas, Nevada
HEIGHT 5 ft 11 in (1.80 in)
WEIGHT 165 lbs (75 kg)
EYES Purple **HAIR** Purple
POWERS With his ionic powers, he has superhuman strength, speed, and resistance to injury. He can fly and project laser beams from his eyes.
ALLIES Avalanche, Headhunter, Shocker, Death Stalker, Scourge
FOES Daredevil, Jessica Jones, Nate Grey, Nick Fury, Captain America

Killgrave's purple skin was caused by a freak chemical mutation.

Pheromones given off by his body can effect more than 100 people standing nearby.

The Purple Man's purple suit enhances his criminal mystique.

PUPPETS ON STRINGS
The Purple Man took on the Thunderbolts, little realizing he was being manipulated by Baron Zemo.

POWER RANK	ENERGY PROJECTION	STRENGTH	DURABILITY	FIGHTING SKILL	INTELLIGENCE	SPEED
	3	2	2	1	2	2

QUAKE

Daisy Johnson is the daughter of the Super Villain Mister Hyde. Given up for adoption at an early age, her power to create strong vibrational waves first manifested itself when the police arrested her for attempted theft. This brought her to the attention of Nick Fury Sr., who persuaded her to join the security agency S.H.I.E.L.D. As Quake, Daisy became a top agent and the leader of Nick Fury's Secret Warriors. She also briefly joined the Avengers.

Quake formerly led the Secret Warriors, a covert team of heroes brought together by Nick Fury Sr. to take on the threat posed by the terrorist group Hydra.

Quake's gloves give her greater control of her powers.

BATTLING ALIEN INVADERS
The Secret Warriors revealed themselves during the Skrull invasion of Earth. Nick Fury Sr. led them into battle against the aliens.

Standard issue S.H.I.E.L.D. equipment belt for use on missions.

Quake wears a standard S.H.I.E.L.D. field uniform

VITAL STATS
REAL NAME Daisy Louise Johnson
OCCUPATION S.H.I.E.L.D. agent
BASE Mobile
HEIGHT 5 ft 4 in (1.63 m)
WEIGHT 115 lbs (52 kg)
EYES Blue **HAIR** Black
POWERS Daisy can generate and control vibrational waves with precision. She can use these to create an earthquake or to rupture a blood vessel in an enemy. She is also trained in martial arts, black ops techniques, and firearms.
ALLIES Nick Fury Sr., Secret Warriors, Avengers
FOES Arnim Zola, Norman Osborn, Hydra

ENERGY PROJECTION	STRENGTH	DURABILITY	FIGHTING SKILL	INTELLIGENCE	SPEED	POWER RANK
5	2	2	6	4	2	

QUASAR

S.H.I.E.L.D. was testing cosmically powered Quantum Bands when agents from A.I.M. (Advanced Idea Mechanics), an organization of power-hungry scientists, tried to steal them. Rookie agent Wendell Vaughn had just failed his S.H.I.E.L.D. exam but was able to use the bands to generate energy and stop A.I.M. He went on to become Quasar, using his powers for the greater good and gaining the title "Protector of the Universe."

Quasar fought alongside Nova during the Skrull invasion of Earth. He also fought alongside the Avengers when they were caught up in a war between the alien Shi'ar and Kree.

VITAL STATS
REAL NAME Wendell Vaughn
OCCUPATION Protector of the Universe
BASE Mobile
HEIGHT 5 ft 10 in (1.77 m)
WEIGHT 180 lbs (81.75 kg)
EYES Blue
HAIR Blond
POWERS Vaughn found that he could control the energy of the Quantum Bands better than any other S.H.I.E.L.D. agent. The bands allow him to fly faster than light speed. They also grant him exceptional strength and the ability to create force fields and fire energy blasts.
ALLIES Nova, Moondragon, Avengers, Fantastic Four
FOES Annihilus, Maelstrom, Ultron

The Quantum Bands were created billions of years ago by Eon, a being who watched over the Universe.

The Bands are made of an unkown metal, and change shape to fit their wearer.

TAKING THE TITLE
When Wendell was believed to be dead, Captain Marvel's daughter, Phyla-Vell assumed his title for a short time.

POWER RANK

ENERGY PROJECTION	STRENGTH	DURABILITY	FIGHTING SKILL	INTELLIGENCE	SPEED
6	4	6	3	3	7

QUICKSILVER

Quicksilver can use his speed to create whirlwinds by running so fast that he stirs up the air around him. He can also move his arms fast enough to fly.

Quicksilver is a mutant speedster and the son of Magneto. He was originally a member of the Brotherhood of Evil Mutants, but reformed and joined the Avengers with his sister, the Scarlet Witch. He married Crystal of the Inhumans and had a daughter, Luna, before divorcing. Quicksilver lost his powers when the Scarlet Witch took away many mutants' abilities on M-Day but they were later restored.

Quicksilver's gray hair is a reflection of his genetic link to Magneto, his father.

Quicksilver is one of the fastest runners on Earth.

Quicksilver convinced his friends and allies that many of his wrongdoings—such as stealing the Terrigen Mists—were the work of a Skrull imposter. Only his daughter, Luna, knows that he lied.

VITAL STATS
REAL NAME Pietro Django Maximoff
OCCUPATION Adventurer
BASE Mobile
HEIGHT 6 ft (1.82 m)
WEIGHT 175 lbs (79.5 kg)
EYES Blue
HAIR Gray/silver
POWERS Quicksilver has the power of super-speed. He is so fast that he is able to run into the future—up to 12 days ahead of the present—until his body tires. The limits of Quicksilver's powers are uncertain.
ALLIES Scarlet Witch, Avengers, Knights of Wundagore
FOES Stranger, Arkon, Brotherhood of Evil Mutants

X-FACTOR
Quicksilver became part of a new X-Factor team led by his younger half-sister Polaris. Gambit was also a member.

ENERGY PROJECTION	STRENGTH	DURABILITY	FIGHTING SKILL	INTELLIGENCE	SPEED
1	4	3	4	3	5

POWER RANK

RADIOACTIVE MAN

When the Chinese government decided to create their own Super Heroes, Doctor Chen Lu exposed himself to nuclear radiation to gain super-powers. He became the Radioactive Man and was sent to the U.S.A. to prove Chinese superiority by beating American heroes. There, he joined the Masters of Evil and fought the Avengers several times. Chen has recently returned to China to be part of the People's Defense Force, China's own Super Hero team.

Radioactive Man was part of a later incarnation of the Thunderbolts alongside Speed Demon, Atlas, Mach IV, Blizzard, and Joystick. He remained with the team following Norman Osborn's takeover.

VITAL STATS

REAL NAME Doctor Chen Lu
OCCUPATION Adventurer
BASE China
HEIGHT 6 ft 6 in (1.98 m)
WEIGHT 290 lbs (131.5 kg)
EYES White **HAIR** None
POWERS The Radioactive Man's body is a living nuclear reactor. He can manipulate all forms of radiation, including heat and hard radiation—with which he can attack his enemies with radiation poisoning, nausea, or dizziness. He can also project energy blasts, create force fields, and induce super-strength in himself.
ALLIES Thunderbolts, Mandarin, Tiberius Stone
FOES Iron Man, Thor, Hank Pym (Wasp II)

His green, glowing skin is the result of radiation.

His costume prevents his radiation from harming those close to him.

BAD INFLUENCE
While working as part of Norman Osborn's version of the Thunderbolts, Chen took on a much deadlier role.

POWER RANK	ENERGY PROJECTION	STRENGTH	DURABILITY	FIGHTING SKILL	INTELLIGENCE	SPEED
	6	4	6	3	5	2

RAGE

Rage and his allies in the New Warriors fought alongside members of the Initiative to help reveal the truth about MVP's death. They later opposed Norman Osborn's takeover of Camp Hammond.

Elvin Haliday was only 12 years old when he jumped into Newtown Creek to escape racist thugs. The chemicals in the river made his body grow into that of a super-strong adult, and his grandmother urged him to use his newfound powers for good. Taking on the name Rage, Elvin fought alongside the Avengers, becoming a member until Captain America learned his real age and asked him to leave the team.

Rage's face mask conceals his identity.

He is still of high school age, but has the body of a super-strong adult.

VITAL STATS
REAL NAME Elvin Daryl Haliday
OCCUPATION Student
BASE Brooklyn, New York City
HEIGHT 6 ft 6 in (1.98 m)
WEIGHT 450 lbs (204 kg)
EYES Brown **HAIR** None
POWERS Rage developed the powers of superhuman speed, reflexes, and durability. He also possesses superhuman strength that increases when used aggressively.
ALLIES Captain America, New Warriors
FOES Sons of the Serpent, Hate-Monger, Doctor Doom

RECKLESS YOUTH
Rage's inexperience sometime leads him into danger—such as the time he attacked Doctor Doom.

Rage is fast enough to outrun an express train.

ENERGY PROJECTION	STRENGTH	DURABILITY	FIGHTING SKILL	INTELLIGENCE	SPEED	POWER RANK
1	6	5	3	2	4	

RAVONNA RENSLAYER

Ravonna is a time-traveling princess from the 40th century. She first opposed Kang the Conqueror but then fell in love with him only to fall into a coma after being shot saving his life. The Grandmaster returned her to health and told her that Kang could have helped her but chose not to. She swore vengeance on Kang, taking the name Terminatrix and attacking his empire across time. The Avengers have often been caught up in her plans.

Ravonna was originally a princess of the small kingdom of Eximietatius in the 40th century. Kang promised to spare the kingdom if Ravonna married him, but she refused.

VITAL STATS

REAL NAME Ravonna Lexus Renslayer
OCCUPATION Princess
BASE Mobile
HEIGHT 5 ft 8 in (1.72 m)
WEIGHT 142 lbs (64.50 kg)
EYES Usually blue, but variable
HAIR Usually blonde, but variable
POWERS Ravonna has enhanced strength, speed, stamina, and agility. She uses advanced technology to alter her appearance. She can teleport, time-travel, and summon versions of herself from different times to help her in a fight. She is highly trained in hand-to-hand combat and has a gifted intellect.
ALLIES Doctor Druid, Carelius
FOES Kang, Avengers, Baltag

Terminatrix has a keen tactical mind.

She wields vibro-knives that can pierce most armor.

Shape-shifting technology allows her to change her appearance at will.

DEADLY CONQUEST
Ravonna was shot and nearly killed saving Kang from Baltag, who had taken over her kingdom by force.

POWER RANK	ENERGY PROJECTION	STRENGTH	DURABILITY	FIGHTING SKILL	INTELLIGENCE	SPEED
	6	4	6	6	3	7

RED GUARDIAN

Alexei Shostakov was the first of several heroes to take on the role of the Red Guardian. He was a highly trained athlete and martial arts expert, and fought the Avengers alongside the Chinese agent Colonel Ling. Shostakov apparently died saving the life of his wife, Black Widow, when Ling tried to shoot her because she had betrayed communism. However, he returned later to try to take her back to Russia on charges of treason. He was stopped by the Widow's Avengers allies.

In a parallel world where Magneto and his family ruled, the Red Guardian was a member of the Winter Guard led by Black Widow. The world was created by the reality altering powers of the Scarlet Witch.

FOR HIS COUNTRY
The Red Guardian helped to defend Russia from Skrulls during their invasion of Earth.

His costume features the Soviet colors and star to inspire fellow Russians.

His belt disc can be thrown as a weapon. It then returns to him by magnetic force.

VITAL STATS
REAL NAME Alexei Shostakov
OCCUPATION Government agent
BASE Moscow
HEIGHT 6 ft 2 in (1.87 m)
WEIGHT 220 lbs (99.75 kg)
EYES Blue **HAIR** Red
POWERS The Red Guardian has exceptional athletic abilities and is a highly skilled martial artist. He was trained by the former Soviet state security organization, the K.G.B., in espionage techniques and advanced hand-to-hand combat.
ALLIES Soviet Super Soldiers
FOES Avengers, Captain America, Alexander Lukin

ENERGY PROJECTION	STRENGTH	DURABILITY	FIGHTING SKILL	INTELLIGENCE	SPEED	POWER RANK
1	2	2	5	3		

RED HULK

For years, General Thunderbolt Ross of the U.S. Air Force hunted the Hulk—only to become one himself! Ross was transformed into the Red Hulk by M.O.D.O.K. and, for a while, appeared to be a villain. In time, Thunderbolt Ross turned on M.O.D.O.K. and the villain's allies in the Intelligencia, fighting against them alongside the Hulk. Red Hulk went on to become a member of the Avengers and later formed his own team of hard-hitting heroes named the Thunderbolts.

Thunderbolt Ross had always hated the Hulk, but when he became the Red Hulk he eventually joined forces with the Hulk and other gamma-spawned heroes in order to save the world.

VITAL STATS

REAL NAME
Thaddeus E. Ross

OCCUPATION Adventurer, former general

BASE Mobile

HEIGHT 7 ft (2.13 m)

WEIGHT 1,200 lbs (544.31 kg)

EYES Yellow **HAIR** Black

POWERS Red Hulk possesses incredible power. The angrier he gets the hotter his body becomes. He can leap great distances and is virtually invulnerable.

ALLIES Hulk, She-Hulk, Red She-Hulk, A-Bomb, Avengers, Thunderbolts

FOES M.O.D.O.K., Intelligencia, Norman Osborn

Red Hulk's grasp of military tactics makes him an asset to any team.

BRAWN AND BRAIN
Red Hulk's military background proved to be a great asset when he joined the Avengers.

Red Hulk's skin can withstand most shells and projectiles.

Red Hulk can absorb radiation to become even stronger.

POWER RANK	ENERGY PROJECTION	STRENGTH	DURABILITY	FIGHTING SKILL	INTELLIGENCE	SPEED
	2	7	6	4	3	3

RED SKULL

The Red Skull was Adolf Hitler's right-hand man and Captain America's archenemy. He was accidentally put in suspended animation near the end of World War II, but was later revived and continued his plans for world domination. At one point the Red Skull infiltrated the U.S. government, unleashing a plague so he could take over the country. Fortunately, the Avengers stopped him.

Arnim Zola created a clone of the Red Skull in World War II that was to be activated in the event of the original's death. The clone stole Professor Xavier's powers and led his S-Men against the Avengers.

Red Skull's Nazi uniform reflects his origins in the Third Reich.

At first he wore a mask, but then an accident with toxic powder made his face a real red skull.

His body is cloned from that of Captain America.

VITAL STATS

REAL NAME Johann Shmidt
OCCUPATION Would-be conqueror
BASE Mobile
HEIGHT 6 ft 1 in (1.85 m)
WEIGHT 195 lbs (88.5 kg)
EYES Blue **HAIR** None
POWERS The Red Skull is a highly trained fighter and marksman, proficient with most firearms. His most powerful advantage over his enemies, however, is his skill as a military and political strategist.
ALLIES Baron Strucker, Arnim Zola
FOES Captain America, Falcon, Avengers

COSMIC CUBE
The Red Skull once gained the Cosmic Cube, which gives its owner the power to change reality itself.

ENERGY PROJECTION	STRENGTH	DURABILITY	FIGHTING SKILL	INTELLIGENCE	SPEED	POWER RANK
1	2	2	6	5	2	

RED WOLF

William Talltrees is the latest Native American to take the name Red Wolf. When William's father was killed by corrupt businessman Cornelius Van Lunt, the Cheyenne god Owayodata gave William super-powers to help him get revenge. He finally brought Lunt to justice in New York, helped by the Avengers. Red Wolf has since fought alongside the team.

Red Wolf is usually accompanied by his wolf, Lobo. The first Lobo died saving his master's life but William adopted a new cub shortly afterward. Man and wolf quickly formed a strong, almost mystical, bond.

VITAL STATS

REAL NAME William Talltrees
OCCUPATION Adventurer
BASE Mobile
HEIGHT 6 ft 4 in (1.93 m)
WEIGHT 240 lbs (108.75 kg)
EYES Dark brown **HAIR** Black
POWERS Red Wolf has superhuman strength and senses. He is extremely fast, an exceptional tracker, and expert horse rider. He can sometimes see visions of the future through meditation.
ALLIES Rangers, Captain America, Firebird, Hawkeye
FOES Texas Twister, Cornelius Van Lunt, Corrupter

Red Wolf's impressive headdress is made from the pelt of his first wolf, Lobo.

Lobo's claws are fitted to Red Wolf's right wrist.

WILD WEST WOLF Johnny Wakely was the Red Wolf in the Wild West of the 19th century.

Red Wolf is skilled with a knife as well as a bow and arrow.

POWER RANK

	ENERGY PROJECTION	STRENGTH	DURABILITY	FIGHTING SKILL	INTELLIGENCE	SPEED
	1	4	2	4	2	2

REPTIL

Reptil can sometimes lose control of himself when he transforms all of his body into a dinosaur—as Avengers Academy teacher Tigra suddenly discovered.

Humberto Lopez found an ancient amulet that gave him the ability to transform any part of his body into that of a dinosaur. The amulet later became embedded in his body. He joined the Avengers Initiative, but was kidnapped by Norman Osborn. After Osborn's downfall, Lopez trained at Avengers Academy. He was taken by Arcade and made to fight other teens. He disappeared after carrying a soon-to-explode Hazmat a safe distance from his friends.

DINOSAUR LINK
During an adventure in the Savage Land, Reptil found himself pitted against real dinosaurs. He can link his mind with theirs.

Reptil can transform his arms into a dinosaur's wings, allowing flight

Reptil can change different parts of his body simultaneously.

VITAL STATS
REAL NAME Humberto Lopez
OCCUPATION Student
BASE Avengers Academy
HEIGHT 5 ft 7 in (1.70 m), but is variable
WEIGHT 142 lbs (64 kg), but is variable
EYES Blue, but is variable
HAIR Black
POWERS Humberto can transform any part of his body into that of a dinosaur—or even his whole body. He can also empathically link with dinosaurs and reptiles.
ALLIES Avengers Academy students, Moon Boy, Ka-Zar, Tigra
FOES Arcade, Norman Osborn, Mentallo, Stegron

ENERGY PROJECTION	STRENGTH	DURABILITY	FIGHTING SKILL	INTELLIGENCE	SPEED
3	4	3	2	2	3

POWER RANK

RICK JONES

Rick Jones was just a teenager when he wandered onto a nuclear test site seconds before a gamma bomb was due to explode. His life was saved by Bruce Banner, who became the Hulk as a result of his act of heroism. Rick felt obliged to help the monster and became a loyal friend to both Bruce and the Hulk. Rick has gained super-powers himself, becoming the Hulk-like Super Hero A-Bomb.

Rick is one of the few people the Hulk considers a friend. It is a friendship that has led Rick into many dangerous situations.

A-BOMB
After years of fighting alongside the Hulk, Rick Jones became the gamma-spawned monster A-Bomb.

VITAL STATS
REAL NAME Rick Jones
OCCUPATION
Adventurer, guitarist
BASE Mobile
HEIGHT 5 ft 9 in (1.75 m)
WEIGHT 185 lbs (84 kg)
EYES Brown **HAIR** Brown
POWERS Until recently, Rick had no powers although he had received combat training from Captain America. As A-Bomb, he possesses Hulk-like strength, speed, and durability, and can track the Hulk by detecting his gamma trail.
ALLIES Hulk, Captain Marvel, Captain America
FOES Red Hulk, Leader, Ares

His body is toned after years of combat training.

For a while, Rick served as Captain America's sidekick.

POWER RANK	ENERGY PROJECTION	STRENGTH	DURABILITY	FIGHTING SKILL	INTELLIGENCE	SPEED
	1	2	2	4	2	2

ROCKET RACCOON

Rocket Raccoon is the most trigger-happy member of the Guardians of the Galaxy. He comes from the planet Halfworld, where animals were genetically altered by robots to take care of the mentally disturbed. Rocket Raccoon escaped the planet and became an adventurer. Arrested by the Kree, he was given the choice of remaining in jail or joining a squad of criminals to attack the evil alien race the Phalanx. This squad became the Guardians of the Galaxy.

Rocket has fought alongside many other intelligent animals, but perhaps the strangest is Cosmo, the Russian space dog. After leaving Earth's atmosphere, Cosmo developed increased intelligence and telepathic abilities.

A REGULAR GUARDIAN
Rocket Raccoon has fought with every incarnation of the present-day Guardians of the Galaxy.

Rocket Raccoon is likely to shoot first and ask questions afterward.

Rocket Raccoon has a large collection of firearms.

VITAL STATS
REAL NAME Rocket Raccoon
OCCUPATION Adventurer
BASE Mobile
HEIGHT 4 ft (1.22 m)
WEIGHT 55 lbs (25 kg)
EYES Brown (sometimes wears blue contact lenses)
HAIR Black, brown, white
POWERS Rocket Raccoon has the abilities of a normal raccoon, such as a heightened sense of smell and sight compared to a human. He is also highly skilled in the use of guns and especially heavy artillery.
ALLIES Guardians of the Galaxy, Avengers
FOES The Badoon, Ultron and the Phalanx

ENERGY PROJECTION	STRENGTH	DURABILITY	FIGHTING SKILL	INTELLIGENCE	SPEED
1	2	2	4	3	2

POWER RANK

RONAN

Ronan was the Supreme Public Accuser of the Kree. When the Fantastic Four destroyed a Kree sentry, he traveled to Earth to punish them, only to be defeated. Returning home in shame, he attempted to take the Empire over but was defeated by Rick Jones when the Avengers became involved in the Kree-Skrull War. Following the events of the Annihilation Wave, Ronan became ruler of the Kree. He re-created the Supreme Intelligence to take his place.

Despite having early doubts, Ronan the Accuser served the Inhumans following their takeover of the Kree Empire.

VITAL STATS

REAL NAME Ronan
OCCUPATION Former ruler
BASE Kree Empire
HEIGHT 7 ft 5 in (2.26 m)
WEIGHT 480 lbs (217.75 kg)
EYES Blue **HAIR** Brown
POWERS He can survive in any environment. His strength-enhancing armor can also make him invisible. He can teleport.
ALLIES Black Bolt, Crystal
FOES Annihilus, Avengers

Ronan's universal weapon can fire energy blasts and create force fields.

ARRANGED MARRIAGE
Ronan's marriage to Crystal was intended to cement an Inhuman/Kree alliance.

He wears the traditional garb of a Kree Supreme Public Accuser.

POWER RANK	ENERGY PROJECTION	STRENGTH	DURABILITY	FIGHTING SKILL	INTELLIGENCE	SPEED
	6	5	6	6	4	7

SANDMAN

Spider-Man is Sandman's archenemy, but the two heroes have also sometimes helped each other. Sandman was even a reserve member of the Avengers until his old ally, the Wizard, turned him evil again.

William Baker has had several identities, but the most notorious was Flint Marko, a thief and gangster. "Flint" was eventually jailed, but he escaped and hid near a nuclear test site. Bombarded by radiation, his body became living sand, and he adopted the name Sandman. At first he used his powers for a criminal career, but he later became a reserve member of the Avengers.

His clothing also turns to sand.

Sandman can shape his body into rock-hard sand, taking on the shape of his choice.

VITAL STATS
REAL NAME William Baker
OCCUPATION Thief
BASE Mobile
HEIGHT 6 ft 1 in (1.85 m)
WEIGHT 240–450 lbs
(108.75–204 kg)
EYES Brown **HAIR** Brown
POWERS He can turn any part of his body into soft or rock-hard sand.
ALLIES The Wizard, Sinister Six, Frightful Four
FOES Spider-Man, Hydro-Man

DOOM'S TEAM
Sandman was once part of a Masters of Evil team created by Doctor Doom.

ENERGY PROJECTION	STRENGTH	DURABILITY	FIGHTING SKILL	INTELLIGENCE	SPEED
1	6	6	4	2	2

POWER RANK

SCARLET WITCH

Wanda Maximoff is a powerful mutant known as the Scarlet Witch who has reshaped reality more than once. The daughter of Magneto, she joined the Avengers with her brother, Quicksilver, in the team's early days. On learning of her lost children (created by magic), Wanda lashed out with her powers, destroying the Avengers Mansion and killing several team members. She eventually rejoined the Avengers seeking redemption for her past actions.

Before joining the Avengers, the Scarlet Witch was a member of the Brotherhood of Evil Mutants. She was not really evil, but served in the Brotherhood out of a sense of duty to Magneto, who had put the team together.

She can only cast hexes on objects in her direct sight.

Throwing hexes requires both mental concentration and ritual gestures.

The Scarlet Witch gets her name from the bright red gown she wears.

VITAL STATS
REAL NAME Wanda Maximoff
OCCUPATION Adventurer
BASE Mobile
HEIGHT 5 ft 7 in (1.70 m)
WEIGHT 132 lbs (60 kg)
EYES Blue **HAIR** Auburn
POWERS She can tap into mystic energy to create reality-altering effects known as hexes. Her powers are entirely natural—sorcery training has given her greater control over them, but there remains a 20 percent chance of error.
ALLIES Vision, Quicksilver, Magneto, Avengers
FOES Master Pandemonium, Mephisto, Annihilus

UNITY SQUAD
The Scarlet Witch was selected to be part of the Avengers Unity squad, made up of both Avengers and X-Men.

POWER RANK	ENERGY PROJECTION	STRENGTH	DURABILITY	FIGHTING SKILL	INTELLIGENCE	SPEED
	6	2	2	3	3	2

SCORPIO

While several people have taken on the role of Scorpio, a member of the criminal Zodiac group, the most infamous was Jake Fury—the younger brother of Nick Fury Sr. For years It was believed Jake had gone bad, using the powerful Zodiac Key to become a major threat to the world. It was later revealed that this Jake Fury was an L.M.D. (Life Model Decoy) and that the real Jake was a hero, gone into deep cover to help Nick bring down Hydra.

Nick Fury Sr. took on the role of Scorpio as cover when he was keeping track of his long lost son, Marcus Johnson.

Scorpion emblem on mask reflects his position as Scorpio in the Zodiac crime cartel.

The Zodiac Key gives its owner vast psionic powers.

VITAL STATS
REAL NAME Jake Fury
OCCUPATION Spy
BASE Mobile
HEIGHT 5 ft 10 in (1.78 m)
WEIGHT 185 lbs (84 kg)
EYES Blue **HAIR** Brown
POWERS Jake Fury was trained in a number of fighting styles. The Zodiac Key that Jake used as Scorpio could fire energy bolts and allowed teleportation.
ALLIES Nick Fury Sr., Avengers, Defenders
FOES Zodiac, Hydra

S.H.I.E.L.D. ENEMIES
Scorpio and his fellow members of the Zodiac were at one point deadly enemies of Nick Fury Sr. and S.H.I.E.L.D.

ENERGY PROJECTION	STRENGTH	DURABILITY	FIGHTING SKILL	INTELLIGENCE	SPEED	POWER RANK
6	3	4	4	5		

SENTRY

Robert Reynolds is the Sentry—one of the Earth's most powerful heroes. Yet this friend and savior to many carries a grim burden. He is also the Void, a dangerous creature that seeks only destruction. The Sentry and his dark alter ego were believed to have been killed during the Siege of Asgard but he later returned, remade by the villainous Apocalypse Twins to be one of their four Horsemen.

The Sentry originally made the world forget he existed. When he returned, he again had to face the Void. He went on to become a proud member of the Avengers before his troubled mind proved no match for the darkness within him.

VITAL STATS
REAL NAME Robert Reynolds
OCCUPATION Adventurer
BASE Mobile
HEIGHT 6 ft (1.82 m)
WEIGHT 194 lbs (88 kg)
EYES Blue **HAIR** Blond
POWERS His abilities include superhuman strength, speed, flight, and invulnerability. However, the full extent of the Sentry's powers have yet to be discovered.
ALLIES Fantastic Four, Avengers, Doctor Strange, Hulk
FOES The Void, Molecule Man

His atoms exist an instant in the future, giving him a state of hyper-consciousness.

A luminescent glow often develops around the Sentry.

DARKNESS REBORN
The Sentry was joined by the Grim Reaper, Banshee, and Daken as the Apocalypse Twins' deadly Horsemen.

POWER RANK	ENERGY PROJECTION	STRENGTH	DURABILITY	FIGHTING SKILL	INTELLIGENCE	SPEED
	3	7	6	2	5	5

SERPENT

The Serpent transformed several heroes and villains into the Worthy, powerful agents of destruction. Sin, transformed into the warrior-god Skadi, was the Worthy's leader.

Cul Borson was the Serpent, the Asgardian god of fear and the older brother of Odin. He was locked away by his fellow Asgardians thousands of years ago but was freed by Sin (the Red Skull's daughter). The Serpent unleashed chaos on the world, with his warriors, known as the Worthy, possessing heroes and villains alike. As fear spread across the Earth, the Serpent became younger and more and more powerful—until his eventual defeat by Thor.

Seemingly old and feeble, the Serpent became younger and more powerful as more fear spread through the world.

The Serpent's staff transformed into a hammer of vast magical power similar to those wielded by the Worthy.

VITAL STATS

REAL NAME Cul Borson
OCCUPATION
Asgardian god of fear
BASE Mobile
HEIGHT 6 ft 2 in (1.87 m)
WEIGHT 230 lbs (104.25 kg)
EYES White
HAIR White (black when young)
POWERS As the son of Bor, Cul's powers rivaled those of Odin himself. As well as amazing strength and the ability to manipulate magic, Cul could feed on people's fear to increase his own power.
ALLIES The Worthy, Sin
FOES Thor, Odin, Asgardian Gods, Avengers, Defenders

THE SWORD OF THOR
Cul transformed into a giant serpent in his last battle with Thor, but was slain by a blow from Thor's magical Odinsword.

ENERGY PROJECTION	STRENGTH	DURABILITY	FIGHTING SKILL	INTELLIGENCE	SPEED	POWER RANK
7	7	7	4	4		

SERSI

Sersi is one of the Eternals, a distant branch of humanity given super-powers by the Celestials. It is thought that she was born in Greece, and she has been involved in many of history's crucial events, from the fall of Camelot to the Crusades. While in the Avengers, Sersi fell in love with the Black Knight. The two Super Heroes traveled through time and parallel worlds together before Sersi was reborn in present day New York.

Sersi was part of an Avengers line-up that included the Black Widow, the Vision, and the Black Knight. Her romantic feelings for the Black Knight caused problems for the team.

VITAL STATS
REAL NAME Sersi
OCCUPATION Adventurer
BASE Mobile
HEIGHT 5 ft 9 in (1.75 m)
WEIGHT 140 lbs (63.5 kg)
EYES Blue
HAIR Black
POWERS Sersi can manipulate cosmic energy to make herself exceptionally strong and nearly invulnerable. She is also virtually immortal.
ALLIES Black Knight, Captain America
FOES Deviants, Proctor

Sersi is able to levitate, fly, and teleport herself.

Although over 5,000 years old, Sersi retains the appearance of a beautiful young woman.

IMMORTAL LOVE
Sersi's bond with the Black Knight led the two heroes to face many foes together.

Her non-super abilities include a talent for fashion design.

POWER RANK	ENERGY PROJECTION	STRENGTH	DURABILITY	FIGHTING SKILL	INTELLIGENCE	SPEED
	7	4	7	2	4	5

SHANG-CHI

Shang-Chi is the Master of Kung Fu. He is the son of a Far Eastern crime lord and was trained from birth to be the world's greatest martial artist—and his father's perfect assassin. However, Shang-Chi refused to follow the evil path intended for him and turned against his father. He has since worked alongside M.I.6. (the U.K.'s top spy organization) to destroy his father's empire and, alone or as part of the Avengers, to help others wherever he can.

Shang-Chi joined forces with Luke Cage, the Black Panther, when his crime lord father's actions threatened the country of Wakanda.

THE SECRET AVENGER
Steve Rogers (Captain America) asked Shang-Chi to join his covert group of heroes dubbed Secret Avengers. Shang-Chi later joined the main Avengers team.

Shang-Chi is highly skilled with all martial arts weaponry.

Metal bracelets help Shang ward off an opponent's blows or weapons.

Shang's ability to harness his mystical *chi* (lifeforce) greatly enhances his physical and mental abilities.

VITAL STATS
REAL NAME Shang-Chi
OCCUPATION Adventurer, secret agent
BASE London, U.K.
HEIGHT 5 ft 10 in (1.78 m)
WEIGHT 175 lbs (78.5 kg)
EYES Brown **HAIR** Black
POWERS Shang-Chi is perhaps the greatest martial artist in the world. His body is honed to physical perfection and his speed and talent are so great he can match superhuman beings in combat.
ALLIES Captain America, Iron Fist, Misty Knight, Tarantula, Colleen Wing
FOES Moving Shadow, the Hand, Shadow Hand, Zaran, Tombstone, Headmen

ENERGY PROJECTION	STRENGTH	DURABILITY	FIGHTING SKILL	INTELLIGENCE	SPEED	POWER RANK
1	2	2	7	3		

SHANNA

Shanna is one of the most respected warriors in the Savage Land and is more than willing to risk her own life to protect the lost wilderness. When she was a child she saw her father accidentally shoot and kill her mother, and since then she has had a distrust of guns. Shanna is married to Ka-Zar, king of the Savage Land, and was saved along with him by the Avengers when the alien Terminus temporarily destroyed the Savage Land. The couple have a son named Matthew.

Shanna needs all her skills to survive the dangers of the Savage Land, but like Ka-Zar she loves the land and fiercely defends it against pollution and interference.

VITAL STATS

REAL NAME Shanna Plunder (née O'Hara)

OCCUPATION Adventurer, ecologist

BASE The Savage Land

HEIGHT 5 ft 10 in (1.77 m)

WEIGHT 140 lbs (63.5 kg)

EYES Hazel **HAIR** Red

POWERS Shanna is an exceptionally agile Olympic-level athlete, as well as a trained veterinarian. She is also highly proficient in the use of knives, spears, and bow and arrows,

ALLIES Ka-Zar, Spider-Man, Avengers, X-Men

FOES Thanos, Terminus, Belasco

Shanna's athletic lifestyle keeps her in tip-top physical condition.

Her costume and wrist guards are made of leather.

Shanna favors hunting weapons such as spears, bows, and knives.

SAVAGE LAND SAVIOR
Shanna once gained cosmic powers and helped to save the Savage Land. The natives worshipped her.

POWER RANK

	ENERGY PROJECTION	STRENGTH	DURABILITY	FIGHTING SKILL	INTELLIGENCE	SPEED
	1	3	2	5	3	2

SHARON CARTER

Sharon Carter not only fought alongside Captain America Steve Rogers on many missions but became romantically involved with him. She even proposed marriage to Cap, but before he could reply, he was whisked away to Dimension Z.

Sharon Carter was inspired to become a S.H.I.E.L.D. operative by stories of her aunt, Peggy Carter, who fought alongside Captain America in World War II. Sharon soon became one of S.H.I.E.L.D.'s finest agents, codenamed Agent 13. She also fought alongside Captain America both as a spy and as a member of the Secret Avengers. She seemingly died in Dimension Z, preventing Arnim Zola's alien forces from invading the Earth, but has now returned.

TEAM PLAYER
When Steve Rogers became security chief, he asked Sharon to join his covert group, the Secret Avengers.

Sharon Carter's costume provides some projectile protection.

Sharon carries a variety of spying equipment and weaponry.

VITAL STATS
REAL NAME Sharon Carter
OCCUPATION Spy, former S.H.I.E.L.D. agent
BASE Mobile
HEIGHT 5 ft 8 in (1.73 m)
WEIGHT 135 lbs (61.25 kg)
EYES Blue **HAIR** Blonde
POWERS An excellent martial artist trained in a variety of spy-craft. Fluent in several languages and an expert with weapons and computers.
ALLIES Captain America, Winter Soldier, Nick Fury Sr., Falcon, Black Widow
FOES Arnim Zola, Red Skull, Sin, Crossbones

ENERGY PROJECTION	STRENGTH	DURABILITY	FIGHTING SKILL	INTELLIGENCE	SPEED
1	2	2	4	3	

POWER RANK

SHE-HULK

When lawyer Jennifer Walters was shot, her cousin Bruce Banner saved her life with a transfusion of his own gamma-irradiated blood. Jennifer soon began to transform into a female Hulk—She-Hulk. Unlike her cousin, Jennifer remains intelligent in Hulk form. She has been a part of the Fantastic Four and the Avengers and still works as a lawyer.

She-Hulk once fled from the Avengers, believing she was a danger to them. When the team tracked her down to the town of Bone, Ohio, she went into a Hulk-like rage, devastating the town. It took the Hulk himself to physically restrain her.

VITAL STATS
REAL NAME Jennifer Walters
OCCUPATION Lawyer, adventurer
BASE New York City
HEIGHT 5 ft 10 (1.77 m) in human form; 6 ft 7 (2 m) in She-Hulk form
WEIGHT 150 lbs (68.5 kg) in human form; 650 lbs (294.75 kg) in She-Hulk form
EYES Green
HAIR Brown (in human form); green (in She-Hulk form)
POWERS As She-Hulk, Jennifer has enormous strength, durability, and a rapid healing factor
ALLIES Man-Wolf, Fantastic Four, Avengers, Hercules, Hellcat
FOES Titania, Absorbing Man

Jennifer's She-Hulk form is less exaggerated than her cousin's.

Her skin is resistant to injury and extremes of temperature.

A formidable martial arts opponent at any time, Jennifer is all but unbeatable in She-Hulk form.

HULK'S LAW
As a lawyer, She-Hulk has taken on many cases involving Super Heroes and Super Villains. She even set up her own firm.

POWER RANK	ENERGY PROJECTION	STRENGTH	DURABILITY	FIGHTING SKILL	INTELLIGENCE	SPEED
	1	7	6	4	3	3

SHOCKER

Herman Schultz was a talented engineer turned expert safecracker. While in prison, he invented a costume that emitted shockwaves, using it to further his criminal career and calling himself Shocker. Profit is his main motivation, and he will work for anyone if the price is right. Shocker joined Egghead's group of villains, Masters of Evil, and was once part of a team Doctor Doom hired to invade Avengers Mansion. He was also part of Boomerang's Sinister Six.

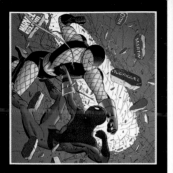

Shocker clashed with Spider-Man the very first time he tried out his battlesuit and gauntlets to commit a crime. Since then, Spidey has become Shocker's nemesis, defeating the villain time and time again.

His shocks can make buildings crumble and human organs disintegrate.

VITAL STATS

REAL NAME Herman Schultz
OCCUPATION Professional thief
BASE New York City
HEIGHT 5 ft 9 in (1.75 m)
WEIGHT 175 lbs (79.25 kg)
EYES Brown **HAIR** Brown
POWERS Vibro-shock units on Shocker's gauntlets use high-pressure air blasts to cause powerful and destructive vibrations. He can produce a continuous shock wave or a series of short blasts, like a flurry of punches. The shock blasts can also be directed at the ground to enable gigantic leaps.
ALLIES Egghead, Doctor Doom, Norman Osborn (Iron Patriot)
FOES Spider-Man, Avengers, Punisher, Captain America

The battlesuit is thickly cushioned to protect Shocker from injury by his own shockwaves.

SHOCK TACTICS
The shockwaves from Shocker's gauntlets stop most opponents in their tracks.

ENERGY PROJECTION	STRENGTH	DURABILITY	FIGHTING SKILL	INTELLIGENCE	SPEED
5	2	5	2	3	

POWER RANK

SILVERCLAW

Lupe Santiago is a daughter of the Volcano Goddess, Peliali. She was raised in an orphanage in the small South American country of Costa Verde, where her shape-shifting powers earned her the name Silverclaw. Jarvis, the Avengers' assistant, was her sponsor and became an uncle-like figure to her. The Avengers aided Silverclaw when the villain Moses Magnum tried to use her abilities for his own ends, and she in turn helped the team when the Scarlet Witch went insane.

In her first meeting with the Avengers, Silverclaw attacked Captain America by mistake. She later teamed up with the Avengers against a sorcerer who was trying to destroy the world.

In action, her skin color becomes silver no matter what animal form she is taking.

When in animal form, she retains some human characteristics.

VITAL STATS
REAL NAME
Maria de Guadalupe "Lupe" Santiago
OCCUPATION
Student
BASE Costa Verde
HEIGHT 5 ft 7 in (1.70 m)
WEIGHT 150 lbs (68 kg)
EYES Brown
HAIR Black with white tips
POWERS Silverclaw can take on the form and abilities of any Costa Verde jungle creature—specific powers depend on the animal. She also has a mystical link to the people of Costa Verde.
ALLIES Iron Man, Avengers, Jarvis
FOES Moses Magnum, Thanos, Ronan

She has taken the form of a jaguar, monkey, and anaconda among others.

BOUND BY DUTY
Silverclaw briefly joined the Avengers but chose to become a reserve member. She felt her first duty was to her homeland.

POWER RANK	ENERGY PROJECTION	STRENGTH	DURABILITY	FIGHTING SKILL	INTELLIGENCE	SPEED
	1	4	3	3	2	3

SIN

Sinthea Shmidt is the Red Skull's daughter. He made sure that she grew up to be violent and brutal. He also speeded up her aging process with his Deus Machina. When she located a hidden Nazi base in the Antarctic, she was taken over by Skadi, a Norse god, and fought alongside the Serpent. Following his defeat by Thor, Sin was left disfigured and became a new Red Skull.

Sin was transformed into Skadi, one of the Worthy (chief agents of the Serpent, transformed by the Serpent's mystical weapons) with power that rivaled Thor's. She freed the Serpent and fought for him until his demise.

A CLOSE CALL FOR CAP
Sin's enhanced powers as Skadi enabled her to come very close to killing Captain America.

Sin is highly trained and expert with all firearms.

Sin carries multiple knives, as deadly, but far quieter, than guns.

Sin is convinced that she can succeed where her father the Red Skull failed and rule the world.

VITAL STATS
REAL NAME Sinthea Shmidt
OCCUPATION Terrorist leader
BASE Mobile
HEIGHT 5 ft 5 in (1.65 m)
WEIGHT 113 lbs (51.25 kg)
EYES Brown
HAIR Brown, dyed red
POWERS Sin is a highly trained killer, practiced in a number of fighting styles. She is experienced with explosives and various weapons, and is an excellent shot.
ALLIES Red Skull, Serpent, Crossbones, Serpent Society
FOES Captain America, Winter Soldier, Sharon Carter

ENERGY PROJECTION	STRENGTH	DURABILITY	FIGHTING SKILL	INTELLIGENCE	SPEED	POWER RANK
1	2	2	4	2	2	

SKAAR

Skaar is the son of the Hulk. He was born on the distant, harsh world of Sakaar, where Hulk had been king and married to Skaar's mother, Caiera. By the time of Skaar's birth, Hulk had returned to Earth. He thought that his wife was dead and was unaware that he had a son. Skaar traveled to Earth, seeking revenge on the father he believed had deserted him and left him to die on Sakaar.

Skaar arrived on Earth wanting to kill his father. However he eventually made peace with the Hulk and fought with him against the Intelligencia, a group of super-intelligent villains.

VITAL STATS

REAL NAME Skaar
OCCUPATION Warrior
BASE Mobile
HEIGHT 6 ft 6 in (1.98 m)
WEIGHT 400 lbs (185.5 kg)
EYES Green **HAIR** Black
POWERS From his father, the Hulk, Skaar inherited gamma-spawned strength. From his mother, he inherited the Old Power, which gives him the ability to increase his strength when touching the ground. He can transform into his childhood self, Shadow, at will.
ALLIES Hulk, A-Bomb, Red She-Hulk, Nick Fury, Moonstone, Trickshot
FOES Norman Osborn, Hiro-Kala, Amatsu-Mikaboshi

Skaar's barbaric appearance recalls his brutal upbringing.

Skaar's massive sword originates on his homeworld of Sakaar.

SECRET SPY
Skaar later joined Norman Osborn's Dark Avengers, working with the team as a double agent for Nick Fury.

POWER RANK	ENERGY PROJECTION	STRENGTH	DURABILITY	FIGHTING SKILL	INTELLIGENCE	SPEED
	2	7	6	4	3	3

SLINGSHOT

Yo Yo Rodriguez is the teenage daughter of the Super Villain Griffin. Unlike her father, Yo Yo decided to use her inherited powers for good. She was recruited by Daisy Johnson for the Secret Warriors but suffered a traumatic injury during an early mission when the villain Gorgon cut off her hands. These were replaced with cybernetic limbs by S.H.I.E.L.D. medics and she has used the extra strength these limbs give her to become an even more powerful hero.

Yo Yo's father, John Horton, was a small-time crook until the subversive group the Secret Empire, using surgery and an experimental serum, transformed him into the Super Villain Griffin. He became a member of crime boss the Hood's gang.

Slingshot wears a standard S.H.I.E.L.D. field uniform

Slingshot has cybernetic hands.

CATCHING ARROWS
Yo Yo's power of super-speed enables her not only to run quickly but gives her lightning-like reactions.

VITAL STATS
REAL NAME Yo Yo Rodriguez
OCCUPATION SH.I.E.L.D. agent
BASE Nick Fury Sr.'s safehouse
HEIGHT Unrevealed
WEIGHT Unrevealed
EYES Brown **HAIR** Black
POWERS Yo Yo's powers give her superhuman speed and allow her to move at super-speed before she slingshots back to her starting point. She also has bionic hands.
ALLIES Nick Fury Sr., Daisy Johnson, Stonewall, Secret Warriors
FOES Gorgon, Hydra, Madame Hydra

ENERGY PROJECTION	STRENGTH	DURABILITY	FIGHTING SKILL	INTELLIGENCE	SPEED	POWER RANK
1	3	2	4	2	5	

SONGBIRD

Melissa Gold was once the villain Screaming Mimi, and used her sonically-enhanced voice to help the Masters of Evil fight the Avengers. She later joined Baron Zemo's Thunderbolts as Songbird but soon turned against Zemo, wishing to fight for justice instead. Norman Osborn tried to kill her, but Nick Fury Sr. helped her to bring him down.

Songbird's voice had already been cybernetically altered before she joined the Masters of Evil. When she became a team member, she received another gift courtesy of the Fixer. It was a harness with beautiful sonic wings that gave her the power of flight.

VITAL STATS

REAL NAME Melissa Joan Gold
OCCUPATION Adventurer
BASE Mobile
HEIGHT 5 ft 5 in (1.65 m)
WEIGHT 145 lbs (65.75 kg)
EYES Green
HAIR Red with white streaks
POWERS Cybernetically enhanced vocal chords allow her to produce sonic blasts that can function as weapons. Her sound waves are able to influence those around her, and her sonic wings enable flight.
ALLIES Nick Fury Sr., Black Widow, MACH 1, Hawkeye (Clint Barton)
FOES Norman Osborn, Bullseye, Graviton

Throat implants enhance her sonic powers.

Her close-fitting costume gives a streamlined shape ideal for flight.

MIMI THE MENACE
As Screaming Mimi, Melissa was a much wilder, more dangerous character. She enjoyed living a life of crime.

Songbird's sonic harness turns sound waves into energy.

POWER RANK

ENERGY PROJECTION	STRENGTH	DURABILITY	FIGHTING SKILL	INTELLIGENCE	SPEED
4	2	6	4	2	3

SPACE PHANTOM

The Space Phantom comes from Limbo, a place where lost souls are trapped and become servants of its ruler, Immortus. The Space Phantom can replace any living person. He takes on their appearance and sends them to Limbo in his place while he imitates them. For years, it was thought the Space Phantom was just one villain but during the Destiny War, the Avengers learned that there are countless Space Phantoms, all identical and living in Limbo awaiting Immortus' orders.

When the Space Phantom impersonated the Hulk, the other Avengers were fooled. This led to the real Hulk leaving the team because he realized that his fellow Avengers were scared of him.

When not impersonating others, all Space Phantoms have the same spooky appearance.

UNTOUCHABLE
Because Thor is a Norse god, he is one of the few beings the Space Phantom cannot replace.

He can take on the powers of objects as well as other beings.

VITAL STATS
REAL NAME Unrevealed
OCCUPATION Servant
BASE Limbo
HEIGHT Unrevealed
WEIGHT Unrevealed
EYES Unknown **HAIR** Black
POWERS He can assume the shape of any creature and take their place so convincingly that no one else will know it is the Space Phantom.
ALLIES Immortus, other Space Phantoms
FOES Avengers, Hulk, Spider-Man

ENERGY PROJECTION	STRENGTH	DURABILITY	FIGHTING SKILL	INTELLIGENCE	SPEED	POWER RANK
1	2	5	2	2	3	

SPECTRUM

Extra-dimensional energy from a terrorist weapon enabled Monica Rambeau to transform into pure energy. She has since had a number of heroic identities. She was dubbed Captain Marvel before changing her name to Photon and then Pulsar. As Spectrum, she has helped Luke Cage and his Mighty Avengers fight off an alien invasion by the mad Titan Thanos' forces.

Monica traveled into space with the Avengers and their cosmic allies during the Kree-Shi'ar war. Her amazing abilities proved to be exceptionally useful during the interstellar conflict, as did her leadership skills.

VITAL STATS
REAL NAME Monica Rambeau
OCCUPATION Adventurer
BASE New York
HEIGHT 5 ft 10 in (1.77 m)
WEIGHT 130 lbs (59 kg)
EYES Brown **HAIR** Black
POWERS Spectrum can transform herself into any form of light within the electromagnetic spectrum, many of which make her intangible and/or invisible. As a ray of light, Photon can fire pulses of energy and fly at speeds up to and including the speed of light.
ALLIES Avengers, Next Wave, Firestar, Black Cat, Hellcat, Spider-Man
FOES Lava Men, Nebula, Moonstone, Blackout

Monica can change her entire body into light.

Monica Rambeau has adventured under various codenames: Captain Marvel, Photon, Pulsar, and Spectrum.

NEW CODENAME
Monica revealed her Spectrum ID while helping Luke Cage's Mighty Avengers fight Thanos' forces.

In her light form, Monica can fly at amazing speeds and even travel through space.

POWER RANK	ENERGY PROJECTION	STRENGTH	DURABILITY	FIGHTING SKILL	INTELLIGENCE	SPEED
	6	2	4	4	3	6

SPEED

Super-powered Tommy Shepherd, alias Speed, was raised as part of a regular family but was sent to Juvenile Hall for accidentally vaporizing his school. He was on the Vision's list of potential Avengers that Iron Lad used to locate his future teammates. Tommy and his teammate Wiccan look like twins, despite having been raised by different families. They are believed to be the long lost magical children of the Scarlet Witch.

Speed and his allies in the Young Avengers teamed up with another team of teenager Super Heroes called the Runaways to fight the alien Skrulls during the Skrull invasion of Earth.

It is possible that Speed's powers come from his uncle, Quicksilver.

VITAL STATS
REAL NAME Thomas "Tommy" Shepherd
OCCUPATION Student
BASE New York City
HEIGHT Unrevealed
WEIGHT Unrevealed
EYES Blue
HAIR White
POWERS Tommy possesses the power to run faster than the speed of sound. He can also produce vibrations that accelerate and disrupt the atoms that make up objects, thereby causing them to explode.
ALLIES Young Avengers, Captain America
FOES Kang, Super Skrull

AVENGING HEROES Speed fought alongside his teammates to protect Asgard from Norman Osborn's attack.

ENERGY PROJECTION	STRENGTH	DURABILITY	FIGHTING SKILL	INTELLIGENCE	SPEED	POWER RANK
3	3	4	2	2		

SPIDER-MAN

Peter Parker became Spider-Man after a bite from an irradiated spider gave him super-powers. At first, Peter used his powers to become a TV star. However, when his actions led to the death of his Uncle Ben, he realized that with great power comes great responsibility. Since then Spider-Man has become a true Super Hero.

Spider-Man first met the Avengers early in his career and fought alongside them several times. He has become an official part of the team and an important and much-loved member.

VITAL STATS

REAL NAME
Peter Benjamin Parker
OCCUPATION Professional photographer, adventurer
BASE New York City
HEIGHT 5 ft 10 in (1.77 m)
WEIGHT 167 lbs (75.75 kg)
EYES Hazel **HAIR** Brown
POWERS Spider-Man can cling to most surfaces and has superhuman strength, speed, and reflexes. A "spider sense" warns him of danger. Web-shooters on his wrists allow him to spray strong web-lines.
ALLIES Fantastic Four, Avengers
FOES Norman Osborn (Green Goblin), Doctor Octopus, Vulture, Sandman

Peter's mask keeps his identity secret.

SUPERIOR SPIDER-MAN
When Doctor Octopus took over Peter Parker's mind, he became a Superior Spider-Man before bringing Peter back to stop the Green Goblin.

Web-shooters create webs to trap bad guys, or ropes that Spidey can swing from.

POWER RANK	ENERGY PROJECTION	STRENGTH	DURABILITY	FIGHTING SKILL	INTELLIGENCE	SPEED
	1	4	3	4	4	3

SPIDER-WOMAN

Spider-Woman was an agent of the criminal organization Hydra before realizing they were evil. After breaking free from their hold, she became a private investigator and fought with the X-Men. Spider-Woman later joined the Avengers; however it emerged that this version of Spider-Woman was a Skrull imposter. The real Spider-Woman has since joined the team.

Early in her career, Spider-Woman was an unwitting agent of Hydra. She even fought Nick Fury on their behalf before becoming a force for good.

SPIDER-WHO?
When Jessica gave up the role of Spider-Woman for a time, several others tried to assume it, including Julia Carpenter.

The collapsible wings are from Jessica's old Hydra costume, although she can now fly without them.

She is able to stun or kill by producing bioelectric blasts.

An adhesive substance secreted from her soles and palms allows her to stick to any surface.

VITAL STATS
REAL NAME Jessica Drew
OCCUPATION Adventurer, private investigator
BASE New York City
HEIGHT 5 ft 10 in (1.77 m)
WEIGHT 130 lbs (59 kg)
EYES Green **HAIR** Black
POWERS Spider-Woman has superhuman strength and speed, and is able to focus her bioelectric energy into "venom blasts" to stun or kill normal humans. She can stick to any surface, and can give off a scent that attracts men and repulses women. She has recently gained the power of flight.
ALLIES Nick Fury Sr., Captain America, Wolverine, Ms. Marvel
FOES Hydra, Morgan Le Fay, Charlotte Winter

ENERGY PROJECTION	STRENGTH	DURABILITY	FIGHTING SKILL	INTELLIGENCE	SPEED	POWER RANK
5	5	4	4	3		

SQUIRREL GIRL

Squirrel Girl is a teenage mutant who, on her first outing as a Super Hero, overwhelmed Doctor Doom with her squirrel army. She later joined the Great Lakes Avengers. Squirrel Girl once had a crush on Speedball (later called Penance) and defeated his foe, the Bug-Eyed Voice. Tragically, her squirrel sidekick, Monkey Joe, was killed by a jealous ex-teammate, but she now has a new favorite squirrel, Tippy-Toe.

Squirrel Girl and her army of squirrels once defeated the mercenary and thief Georges Batroc, a.k.a. the Leaper. Other villains she has defeated include the Bug-Eyed Voice, Thanos, M.O.D.O.K., Giganto, and Deadpool.

VITAL STATS

REAL NAME Doreen Green

OCCUPATION Student, adventurer

BASE Milwaukee, Wisconsin

HEIGHT 5 ft 3 in (1.60 m)

WEIGHT 100 lbs (45.5 kg)

EYES Brown **HAIR** Brown

POWERS Squirrel Girl possesses enhanced strength, speed, and reflexes. She has small retractable claws, enlarged incisor teeth, and a prehensile tail. She also has an empathic bond with her squirrel sidekicks and the ability to talk to squirrels in general.

ALLIES Great Lakes Avengers, Hawkeye, Mockingbird, Tippy-Toe

FOES Doctor Doom, Maelstrom, the Bug-Eyed Voice

She uses squirrel sounds to talk to her furry pals.

Her prehensile tail is a mutant characteristic.

Her belt has pouches for stores of nuts, which give her extra energy.

TIME OUT When not fighting crime, Doreen likes to spend time relaxing with her favorite squirrels.

POWER RANK	ENERGY PROJECTION	STRENGTH	DURABILITY	FIGHTING SKILL	INTELLIGENCE	SPEED
	1	4	3	4	2	3

STAR BRAND

Kevin Connor became the Star Brand when the mysterious White Event hit Earth. The energy of his change into Star Brand devastated his college, killing thousands of students. When the Avengers came to investigate, a confused but cosmically powerful Kevin fought with the heroes before making peace and being invited to join the team. Since then, his powers have proved an invaluable asset.

Despite their initial violent confrontation, Star Brand (Kevin Connor) soon joined the Avengers. He did so on the advice of Captain Universe.

Star Brand gives the bearer infinite power, limited only by the bearer's own imagination.

Kevin Conner wears the symbol of the Star Brand on his chest.

VITAL STATS
REAL NAME Kevin Connor
OCCUPATION
Super Hero, student
BASE Avengers Tower
HEIGHT Unrevealed
WEIGHT Unrevealed
EYES Blue **HAIR** Blond
POWERS The Star Brand grants its bearer cosmic powers. It also grants invulnerability, the power of flight, and the ability to unleash bolts of powerful energy. He can also travel faster than the speed of light.
ALLIES Nightmask, Avengers, Captain Universe
FOES Thanos, the Builders

IN ANOTHER UNIVERSE
Kenneth Connell became the Star Brand in another universe, using the power to protect his own version of Earth.

ENERGY PROJECTION	STRENGTH	DURABILITY	FIGHTING SKILL	INTELLIGENCE	SPEED	POWER RANK
7	2	3	1	2	2	

STARFOX

Eros is the youngest son of Mentor, the ruler of a group of Eternals living on Titan. Eros loves life and pleasure, unlike his older brother Thanos, who is obsessed with death.

When Eros first joined the Avengers, the original Wasp suggested that he use the name Starfox because it sounded more heroic than Eros. Since then, Starfox has proved to be a popular member of the team.

Eros was born on Titan, one of Saturn's moons. He was a famous mythical figure on Earth long before he joined the Avengers and became Starfox. Starfox's scientific knowledge is very important to the Avengers.

VITAL STATS
REAL NAME Eros
OCCUPATION Adventurer
BASE Titan
HEIGHT 6 ft 1 in (1.85 m)
WEIGHT 190 lbs (86 kg)
EYES Blue **HAIR** Red
POWERS Starfox can create feelings of pleasure and delight in those around him. He can harness cosmic energy and reuse it as energy blasts. He is superhumanly strong and ages far more slowly than most humanoids. Starfox can also survive in deep space and the ocean, and has the power of flight.
ALLIES Genis-Vell, Eternals, Avengers
FOES Thanos, Super Skrull, Morgan Le Fay

Starfox can speak over 500 alien languages.

He can surround himself with an invisible force field that enables him to travel through space and underwater.

LOSING HIS CHARM
Starfox used his powers to make She-Hulk marry John Jameson, and she beat him up when she found out.

POWER RANK	ENERGY PROJECTION	STRENGTH	DURABILITY	FIGHTING SKILL	INTELLIGENCE	SPEED
	3	4	3	3	3	5

STARHAWK

Stakar shares the Starhawk identity with his adopted sister, Aleta Ogord. While the two usually operate in harmony, they have been known to fall out, with each trying to dominate the Starhawk power.

Stakar Ogord is the son of Super Heroes Quasar and Kismet from an alternate timeline. He received cosmic powers from the hawk god of the planet Arcturus and, as Starhawk, helped the Guardians of the Galaxy defeat the Badoon in the 31st century. He fought alongside the Avengers against Korvac and has helped the modern-day Guardians of the Galaxy.

Starhawk creates photons—tiny particles of light—which enable him to fly. He can generate light to illuminate the way ahead or to blind an opponent.

Starhawk's suit has a retracting, transparent facemask, a life-support system, and retractable wings.

VITAL STATS
REAL NAME Stakar Ogord
OCCUPATION Adventurer
BASE Mobile
HEIGHT 6 ft 4 in (1.93 m)
WEIGHT 450 lbs (204 kg)
EYES White, with no visible pupils
HAIR Brown
POWERS Starhawk can generate luminous energy, either as a glow or concentrated into blasts of exceptional heat and power. He is also able to use photons to move at great speed.
ALLIES Guardians of the Galaxy, Defenders, Avengers
FOES Badoon, Korvac

JUST IN TIME
Starhawk traveled back from the 31st century to the present to protect the world from Korvac.

ENERGY PROJECTION	STRENGTH	DURABILITY	FIGHTING SKILL	INTELLIGENCE	SPEED	POWER RANK
5	4	3	2	4	7	

STAR-LORD

Peter Quill is Star-Lord, leader of the Guardians of the Galaxy. Born on Earth, his mother was killed by alien Badoon when he was still young and he never knew his father. He later learned that his father was J-son, ruler of the Spartax Empire. Peter joined N.A.S.A. and traveled into space seeking revenge on the Badoon who killed his mother. He became a founding member of the modern-day incarnation of the Guardians of the Galaxy, the team he continues to lead.

Star-Lord first suggested the Guardians of the Galaxy stay together after they helped to stop Ultron and the Phalanx from conquering the universe.

VITAL STATS

REAL NAME Peter Quill
OCCUPATION Adventurer
BASE Mobile
HEIGHT 6 ft 2 in (1.88 m)
WEIGHT 175 lbs (79.5 kg)
EYES Blue **HAIR** Blond
POWERS Star-Lord is an excellent tactician and fighter, experienced with firearms from all over the galaxy. His suit includes rocket boots and a helmet that allows him to breathe in space. He favors a powerful element gun in combat.
ALLIES Groot, Gamora, Mantis, Rocket Raccoon, Drax, Angela, X-Men
FOES J-son, Badoon, Thanos, Ultron, Phalanx

Star-Lord has an element gun, a pistol that can project blasts of one of the four elements.

Star-Lord's helmet enables him to breathe in outer space.

FATHER AND SON
Star-Lord's father is King J-son of the Spartax Empire. Peter blames his father for his mother's death and sees him as an uncaring dictator.

POWER RANK

ENERGY PROJECTION	STRENGTH	DURABILITY	FIGHTING SKILL	INTELLIGENCE	SPEED
1	3	3	4	4	2

STATURE

As part of the Young Avengers, Cassie fought the Young Masters, a team of evil super-powered teens. The Young Masters, who based their name on the Masters of Evil Super Villain team, were soundly defeated.

Cassie Lang was the daughter of Scott Lang, the second Ant-Man. Cassie's father was a member of the Avengers and, growing up, she spent time with the team. Cassie always wanted to be a Super Hero like her father, so after his apparent death, she took Pym Particles and gained size-changing abilities. Cassie became a member of the Young Avengers only to be killed by Doctor Doom after saving her father's life.

Cassie's costume was based on her father's Ant-Man costume.

SKRULL WAR
Cassie fought alongside many Super Heroes and Super Villains against the Skrulls during their invasion of Earth.

The costume grew or shrank in size along with Cassie.

VITAL STATS
REAL NAME Cassandra "Cassie" Eleanore Lang
OCCUPATION Student
BASE New York City
HEIGHT Variable
WEIGHT Variable
EYES Blue **HAIR** Blonde
POWERS Cassie had the power to grow or shrink her body just like her father, Ant-Man. Her powers were connected to her emotions, however, and she had been known to shrink if embarrassed.
ALLIES Young Avengers, Hank Pym, Fantastic Four
FOES Kang, Super Skrull, Norman Osborn (Iron Patriot)

ENERGY PROJECTION	STRENGTH	DURABILITY	FIGHTING SKILL	INTELLIGENCE	SPEED	POWER RANK
1	5	4	3	2	2	

STINGRAY

Doctor Walter Newell is an oceanographer. He created his Stingray costume when the government forced him to capture the Sub-Mariner, who was thought to be aiding aliens. Stingray succeeded, but released the Sub-Mariner after becoming convinced of his innocence. He later came into contact with the Avengers when the team moved its base to the seacraft/island Hydrobase, where Newell had his lab. He joined the Avengers on several missions and was part of the Avengers Initiative.

Iron Man once believed Stingray's costume was created from his own stolen technology. He was mistaken, and the two heroes are now friends.

VITAL STATS

REAL NAME Doctor Walter Newell
OCCUPATION Oceanographer
BASE Mobile
HEIGHT 6 ft 3 in (1.90 m)
WEIGHT 200 lbs (90.75 kg)
EYES Hazel **HAIR** Brown
POWERS Stingray's armored suit allows him to survive in the deepest oceans. It enables underwater breathing while also providing superhuman strength and speed. The armor can also produce powerful electrical blasts.
ALLIES Sub-Mariner, Thing, Avengers
FOES Master of the World, Kang, Lava Men, Tiger Shark

Breathing apparatus allows Stingray to spend unlimited time underwater.

SEA STRUGGLE
Although Stingray and the Sub-Mariner fought each other, it was a misunderstanding and they have since become allies.

Wings allow flight and increase speed underwater.

POWER RANK	ENERGY PROJECTION	STRENGTH	DURABILITY	FIGHTING SKILL	INTELLIGENCE	SPEED
	4	4	4	2	4	3

STRANGER

The Stranger and several other powerful beings, including Galactus, were once captured by Thanos when the mad Titan gained possession of the Infinity Gauntlet.

The Stranger possesses the combined strength and intelligence of the billions of people who once lived on the planet Gigantus. They all joined together as one being to defeat an alien called the Overmind who was threatening their planet. The Stranger is fascinated by Earth and its super-powered beings, and has taken some away to examine. He has even teamed with them, once helping the Avengers to defeat Nebula.

The Stranger can change his size and shape at will.

The Stranger is an enigmatic being. No one is really sure what motivates him.

VITAL STATS
REAL NAME Unknown
OCCUPATION Scientist
BASE Mobile
HEIGHT Variable
WEIGHT Variable
EYES Black **HAIR** White
POWERS The Stranger possesses cosmic and psionic powers beyond human measurement. He is able to alter his shape and size at will, manipulate gravity so that he can levitate, and move across the cosmos almost instantly, taking others with him. He can also emit powerful energy blasts and erect impenetrable force fields.
ALLIES None
FOES Overmind, Magneto, Pluto

STAR SPANNER
The Stranger can send an image of himself across an entire galaxy to communicate with people.

ENERGY PROJECTION	STRENGTH	DURABILITY	FIGHTING SKILL	INTELLIGENCE	SPEED	POWER RANK
7	7	6	2	7	7	

STRIKER

Brandon Sharpe's mother pushed him into becoming a child actor. When his manager attacked him, Brandon discovered that he had the ability to generate and control vast amounts of electricity and became Striker. Striker's difficult upbringing means that he comes across as arrogant and egocentric. His trainers at Avengers Academy worry that, following experimentation at the hands of Norman Osborn and his colleagues, he may turn to evil.

Striker has used his power to increase his own fame. Before being captured by Norman Osborn, he often appeared on stage and TV.

VITAL STATS

REAL NAME Brandon Sharpe
OCCUPATION Student
BASE Avengers Academy
HEIGHT Unrevealed
WEIGHT Unrevealed
EYES Blue **HAIR** Black
POWERS Striker can collect and control electrical energy and emit it in energy blasts. He can also use this energy to fly. His targeted use of his powers is excellent as he believes accidental casualties will damage his public standing.
ALLIES Fellow students at Avengers Academy, Julie Power
FOES Whirlwind, the Hood, Psycho Man, Korvac

Striker's face was scarred fighting the Super Villain Jeremy Briggs.

Striker's flashy costume is designed to ensure maximum media impact.

SHARP SHOCKS
At Avengers Academy, Striker clashed with the young Runaways, whose parents were Super Villains.

POWER RANK	ENERGY PROJECTION	STRENGTH	DURABILITY	FIGHTING SKILL	INTELLIGENCE	SPEED
	5	2	2	3	3	2

SUB-MARINER

The Sub-Mariner can control massive creatures that live in the ocean depths. He summons them with the Horn of Proteus, a relic from Atlantis.

Namor the Sub-Mariner is the child of a human father and an Atlantean mother and the ruler of the underwater kingdom of Atlantis. Although initially hostile toward surface dwellers, the Sub-Mariner ended up fighting alongside Captain America against the Nazis during World War II and has done so again as a member of the Avengers. His first loyalty, however, is to Atlantis and he will fight anyone to protect it—even those he considers allies and friends.

The gills behind his ears enable him to breathe underwater.

VITAL STATS
REAL NAME Namor McKenzie
OCCUPATION King of Atlantis
BASE Atlantis
HEIGHT 6 ft 2 in (1.87 m)
WEIGHT 278 lbs (126 kg)
EYES Blue/gray **HAIR** Black
POWERS He has super-strength (increased further when in water), superhuman stamina, speed, and durability. Fin-like wings on his ankles enable him to fly. He can see clearly even in the darkness of the deep ocean, and can breathe on land and underwater. He also has a telepathic rapport with most marine animals.
ALLIES Captain America, Hulk, Human Torch, Fantastic Four, Doctor Strange
FOES Tiger-Shark, Nitro, Attuma

BATTLING BUCKY
When Bucky Barnes replaced Steve Rogers as Captain America, he clashed with the Sub-Mariner.

The Sub-Mariner can swim at speeds of up to 60 miles per hour (96.6 km/h).

ENERGY PROJECTION	STRENGTH	DURABILITY	FIGHTING SKILL	INTELLIGENCE	SPEED
2	6	6	4	2	

POWER RANK

SUPER-ADAPTOID

The Super-Adaptoid contains a sliver of the reality-altering Cosmic Cube and was created by A.I.M. to destroy Captain America. It outgrew its programming and started to act independently, taking on the powers of the Avengers when clashing with them. It has also fought the original X-Men and the Fantastic Four. After several defeats, the Super-Adaptoid was made part of the Phalanx but maintained some independence from the Phalanx's hive mind.

When Ultron and the Phalanx were seeking to take over the universe, the Super-Adaptoid was brought into the Phalanx and fought against Phyla-Vell, the daughter of Captain Mar-Vell.

VITAL STATS

REAL NAME Super-Adaptoid
OCCUPATION Criminal
BASE Mobile
HEIGHT 6 ft 2 in (1.88 m), but is variable
WEIGHT 210 lbs (95.25), but is variable
EYES Black **HAIR** None
POWERS The Super-Adaptoid can copy the powers and appearance of up to eight super-powered beings at a time (it turns green while doing so). It can also alter its size and shape.
ALLIES Madame Masque, Legion of the Unliving
FOES Avengers, X-Men, Fantastic Four

The Super-Adaptoid takes on part of the appearance—such as Iron Man's armor—of whomever it copies.

Its body contains a fragment of the powerful Cosmic Cube.

POWER GRAB
During the Super-Adaptoid's first battle with the Avengers, it took on all the Avengers' mighty powers.

The Super-Adaptoid's high power rank reflects his adaptation potential.

	ENERGY PROJECTION	STRENGTH	DURABILITY	FIGHTING SKILL	INTELLIGENCE	SPEED
POWER RANK	7	7	7	7	2	7

SUPREME INTELLIGENCE

The Supreme Intelligence is an organic, artificial creature. He was created by the alien Kree to house the combined intellect and experience of their greatest minds. During the first Kree-Skrull War, the Supreme Intelligence manipulated Rick Jones and Captain Marvel in an attempt to restart Kree evolution. He has been presumed dead several times—once after being killed by the Avengers—but has always found a way to return and regain control of the Kree.

As the ruler of the Kree Empire, the Supreme Intelligence had a vast legion of soldiers and henchmen to call upon.

DOMINATION SUPREME
The Supreme Intelligence's plans for conquest have often brought him into conflict with the Avengers.

The Supreme Intelligence has vast psychic abilities.

His artificial mind is kept alive by advanced technology.

VITAL STATS
REAL NAME Supreme Intelligence
OCCUPATION Former leader of the Kree
BASE Mobile
HEIGHT 25 ft (7.62 m), but is variable
WEIGHT 544,000 lbs (264,754 kg), but is variable
EYES Yellow **HAIR** None, but has green tentacles on his head
POWERS He possesses great psychic abilities, the full extent of which is as yet unknown.
ALLIES Kree
FOES Avengers, Skrulls, Shi'ar

ENERGY PROJECTION	STRENGTH	DURABILITY	FIGHTING SKILL	INTELLIGENCE	SPEED	POWER RANK
6	4	3	6	6	2	

SWORDSMAN

The original Swordsman was Jacques Duquesne, who had trained Hawkeye (Clint Barton). Although he was a villain at first, Swordsman became a force for good after falling in love with Mantis, and eventually died to save the Avengers and Mantis from Kang the Conqueror. He was later resurrected and married Mantis, but he became possessed by an alien and died again in a fight with the Avengers.

A new incarnation of the Swordsman was a member of the Thunderbolts. He remained with the team of reformed Super Villains for several missions before he was eventually killed by Venom.

DEAD ALLIES
The Swordsman found himself briefly back from the dead and fighting with other deceased Avengers against the Grim Reaper.

His modified sword can fire energy blasts, lightning, and stun gas.

Swordsman is also adept with a knife, which he carries as back-up in case he loses his sword in battle.

VITAL STATS
REAL NAME Jacques Duquesne
OCCUPATION Mercenary, adventurer
BASE Mobile
HEIGHT 6 ft 4 in (91.93 m)
WEIGHT 250 lbs (113.5 kg)
EYES Blue **HAIR** Black
POWERS Swordsman wields a sword modified by the Super Villain Mandarin to shoot out lightning, fire, stun gas, and various energy blasts.
ALLIES Mantis, Hawkeye, Avengers (former foe)
FOES Enchantress (former ally), Power Man (former ally)

POWER RANK	ENERGY PROJECTION	STRENGTH	DURABILITY	FIGHTING SKILL	INTELLIGENCE	SPEED
	6	2	2	6	2	2

TASKMASTER

Taskmaster has fought many heroes, including Spider-Man. He is able to replicate any hero's fighting style exactly. He can also combine it with the skills of other heroes he has faced, giving him an important advantage!

Taskmaster can rcmember any move he sees, and has used this power to become a sought-after mercenary. However, he was defeated by the Avengers despite being able to mimic all their fighting styles. After years of living on the wrong side of the law, Taskmaster became a government agent during the Super Hero Civil War and was a teacher at Camp Hammond before going on to join the Secret Avengers.

Taskmaster uses an image inducer to replace his true face with any other person's.

A metal alloy shield doubles as a throwing weapon.

His utility belt holds an array of weapons.

VITAL STATS
REAL NAME Unrevealed
OCCUPATION Mercenary, drill instructor
BASE Mobile
HEIGHT 6 ft 2 in (91.87 m)
WEIGHT 220 lbs (99.75 kg)
EYES Unrevealed **HAIR** Brown
POWERS Taskmaster possesses photographic reflexes, which enable him to watch another person's movements and duplicate them. He has mastered many martial arts by duplicating actions seen in movies. He also has a photographic memory and can copy a person's voice.
ALLIES Norman Osborn, Wizard, Constrictor, Red Skull
FOES Captain America, Daredevil, Moon Knight, the Punisher

COVERT ATTACK
Taskmaster infiltrated A.I.M. for Nick Fury's covert Avengers team, helping fight their creations.

ENERGY PROJECTION	STRENGTH	DURABILITY	FIGHTING SKILL	INTELLIGENCE	SPEED	POWER RANK
1	3	2	7	4		

THANOS

Thanos is a Titan of immense power. He once met Death and, perceiving it in a female form, became obsessed with winning her love—even if it meant destroying the universe to impress her. Thanos has been stopped and even killed but always returns stronger and more deadly than ever. He formed the Cull Obsidian and came close to conquering the Earth before the Avengers and their allies, including Thanos' son, Thane, managed to stop him.

Thanos once gained the Infinity Gauntlet, an item of enormous power. Its six Infinity Gems gave control over time, space, reality, and the souls of others, unlimited strength, and psychic powers.

His mind is highly resistant to psychic attack.

VITAL STATS
REAL NAME Thanos
OCCUPATION Conqueror
BASE Mobile
HEIGHT 6 ft 7 in (2 m)
WEIGHT 985 lbs (446.75 kg)
EYES Red
HAIR None
POWERS Thanos possesses superhuman strength, endurance, and reflexes. He is almost invulnerable, and can project energy blasts from his hands and mind.
ALLIES Death
FOES Starfox, Warlock, Captain Marvel

Thanos' strength has been enhanced by biological augmentation and magic.

DEATH DEALER
Thanos' obsession with Death has led him to kill billions.

POWER RANK	ENERGY PROJECTION	STRENGTH	DURABILITY	FIGHTING SKILL	INTELLIGENCE	SPEED
	6	7	6	4	6	3

THOR

Thor is one of the greatest of the Norse gods, and lives with them in Asgard. He grew up with his half-brother Loki, who was always jealous of Thor's position as the powerful, favored son of Odin.

Thor is the Norse god of thunder. When his father, Odin, thought Thor was becoming too proud, he cast him down to Earth in the form of the lame Doctor Donald Blake. However, Blake found a walking stick and was transformed back into Thor, the walking stick turning into his hammer, Mjolnir. Thor was a founding member of the Avengers and remains one of Earth's greatest protectors. While others have taken on the role, he has always eventually reclaimed it.

THE NEW THOR
Thor was replaced with a new female god of thunder who also took his name.

Mjolnir is almost unbreakable.

The Belt of Strength doubles Thor's strength during battle, although it leaves him weakened afterwards.

Thor's body is much denser than human flesh and bone.

VITAL STATS
REAL NAME Thor Odinson
OCCUPATION Prince of Asgard, god of thunder
BASE Asgard
HEIGHT 6 ft 6 in (1.98 m)
WEIGHT 640 lbs (290.25 kg)
EYES Blue
HAIR Blond
POWERS He has immense strength and durability, and can control thunder and lightning. With Mjolnir he can fly and open portals to other dimensions.
ALLIES Warriors Three, Captain America, Beta Ray Bill
FOES Surtur, Loki, Absorbing Man, Wrecking Crew

ENERGY PROJECTION	STRENGTH	DURABILITY	FIGHTING SKILL	INTELLIGENCE	SPEED	POWER RANK
6	7	6	4	2		

THOR GIRL

Tarene was originally born on an alien world. She first met Thor, the Norse god of thunder, when he helped her avenge the destruction of her homeworld by the mad Titan Thanos. Tarene was so impressed by Thor that she turned herself into an Asgardian and became his ally, known as Thor Girl. She fought alongside the Avengers when the Hulk threatened New York. Thor Girl was also part of the Initiative.

Thor Girl bravely took on Ragnarok when Thor was reanimated as a cyborg-clone. Defeated, but saved by the New Warriors, Thor Girl left to find and warn the true Thor.

VITAL STATS
REAL NAME Tarene
OCCUPATION Adventurer
BASE Camp Hammond
HEIGHT 5 ft 9 in (1.75 m)
WEIGHT 317 lbs (143.75 kg)
EYES Blue **HAIR** Blonde
POWERS Thor Girl possesses amazing strength and invulnerability. As an Asgardian goddess, she is ageless. Her mystic hammer is not only a powerful physical weapon—it can also be used to fire energy blasts, control the weather, and enable Thor Girl to fly.
ALLIES Thor, Justice, Ultra Girl
FOES The Serpent, Skrulls, Thanos

Striking her hammer on the ground enables Thor Girl to assume human form and change back again.

Thor Girl can use her hammer as a weapon. When she throws it at an opponent, it always comes back to her.

FIGHTING FEAR
When the Serpent and his followers attacked Earth, Thor Girl led her fellow students into battle against them.

POWER RANK	ENERGY PROJECTION	STRENGTH	DURABILITY	FIGHTING SKILL	INTELLIGENCE	SPEED
	6	5	4	3	2	3

3-D MAN

Delroy thought his powers had been unlocked by the Triune. He became their spokesman and fought alongside the Avengers before learning that the Triune was using him to undermine the Super Hero team.

Delroy Garrett is the second 3-D Man. The failed athlete was given super-powers by the Triune, a sinister self-development organization, so that he could help them discredit the Avengers. When Delroy (then known as Triathlon) learned of the Triune's evil intentions, he turned against them to save the Avengers. He also found out that his powers had been stolen from the original 3-D Man, so he took that name to honor his predecessor.

3-D Man's goggles can see disguised Skrulls for what they really are.

Delroy maintains his athletic body through regular training.

Delroy's costume is an updated version of the one used by the original 3-D Man.

VITAL STATS
REAL NAME Delroy Garrett
OCCUPATION Adventurer
BASE Mobile
HEIGHT 6 ft 2 in (1.87 m)
WEIGHT 200 lbs (90.75 kg)
EYES Brown **HAIR** Black
POWERS His strength, speed, stamina, and senses are approximately three times higher than the upper limits of human ability. His body contains the "Tri-Force," an energy that he can channel through his eyes to see Skrulls.
ALLIES Initiative, Skrull Kill Krew, Avengers
FOES Triune, Skrulls

SEEING SKRULLS
3-D Man could see alien Skrulls disguised as Super Heroes and joined the Skrull Kill Krew to fight them.

ENERGY PROJECTION	STRENGTH	DURABILITY	FIGHTING SKILL	INTELLIGENCE	SPEED
1	4	3	4	2	

POWER RANK

THUNDERSTRIKE

When architect Eric Masterson nearly died saving Thor, Odin merged the two men to save Eric's life. Eric and Thor shared one body until Thor was banished from Asgard, and Eric, now in sole control of the body, found himself taking Thor's place. Odin gave him Thor's powers and a hammer, Thunderstrike, after which Eric named himself. He replaced Thor in the Avengers, but died saving the world from the Bloodaxe curse.
His son, Kevin, became the new Thunderstrike.

As Thunderstrike, Eric became a regular member of the Avengers, traveling to the future with the team to fight the time-traveling Super Villain Terminatrix.

VITAL STATS
REAL NAME Eric Kevin Masterson
OCCUPATION Architect, adventurer
BASE Asgard
HEIGHT 6 ft 6 in (1.98 m)
WEIGHT 640 lbs (290.25 kg)
EYES Blue
HAIR Blond
POWERS Thunderstrike possessed superhuman strength and stamina, and wielded an enchanted hammer called Thunderstrike that could emit blasts of energy and flashes of light. It also enabled him to fly.
ALLIES Thor, Avengers
FOES Bloodaxe, Mongoose

His costume is based on that of Thor.

Thunderstrike's hammer was made especially for him by the Norse gods.

GRIM LEGION
After his death, Thunderstrike joined the Legion of the Unliving in an attack on the Avengers.

POWER RANK	ENERGY PROJECTION	STRENGTH	DURABILITY	FIGHTING SKILL	INTELLIGENCE	SPEED
	5	5	6	3	2	5

THUNDRA

Thundra is one of the world's mightiest females. She often teams up with other formidable female Super Heroes, and once fought alongside Valkyrie and She-Hulk ito try and stop the Red Hulk's rampage.

Thundra is a powerful warrior woman from a future where men and women are at war with each other. She was sent back in time to defeat the greatest male warriors of the present day. Despite her dislike of men, Thundra became a friend of Hyperion and came into conflict with the Avengers when Hyperion's team, the Squadron Sinister, fought them. Thundra recently helped the Red Hulk escape from the Intelligencia, a villainous group of geniuses, before returning to her own time.

A DAUGHTER FOR THUNDRA
Thundra became pregnant using some of Hulk's cells. Their daughter Lyra has started to call herself She-Hulk.

The chain weapon attached to her bracelet can also be worn as a belt.

Genetic engineering and years of training have given Thundra formidable strength and stamina.

VITAL STATS
REAL NAME Thundra
OCCUPATION Warrior
BASE Mobile
HEIGHT 7 ft 2 in (2.18 m)
WEIGHT 350 lbs (158.75 kg)
EYES Green
HAIR Red
POWERS Thundra possesses superhuman strength, endurance, and durability as a result of genetic engineering. She is also a highly trained warrior, specializing in the use of a three-foot chain as a weapon.
ALLIES Arkon, Valkyrie, Red Hulk, Thing
FOES Mahkizmo, Mad Thinker, Nth Man

ENERGY PROJECTION	STRENGTH	DURABILITY	FIGHTING SKILL	INTELLIGENCE	SPEED
1	5	6	4	2	2

POWER RANK

TIGER SHARK

As ferocious and deadly as he sounds, Tiger Shark was formerly Todd Arliss, an Olympic swimmer. After an accident ended his swimming career, Arliss' genetic structure was mixed with that of a tiger shark and the Sub-Mariner. A sworn enemy of both the Sub-Mariner and his ally Stingray, Tiger Shark became a member of Egghead's Super Villain group, Masters of Evil, fighting the Avengers several times. He has also been a member of the Lethal Legion.

At first Tiger Shark was a superhuman, amphibious creature, but he later mutated further. Norman Osborn once hired the mutated Tiger Shark to hunt and kill the mercenary Deadpool. Tiger Shark came close to killing the mercenary, but was eventually defeated.

VITAL STATS

REAL NAME Todd Arliss
OCCUPATION Criminal
BASE Mobile
HEIGHT 6 ft 1 in (1.85 m)
WEIGHT 450 lbs (204 kg)
EYES Gray **HAIR** Brown
POWERS Arliss' body has been surgically and genetically altered to give him shark-like abilities. He has superhuman strength and endurance and is able to swim up to 60 miles per hour (96.6 km/h). His strength is at its greatest when in contact with water, so when on land he wears a costume with a water circulation system built into it.
ALLIES Egghead, Baron Zemo
FOES Sub-Mariner, Hank Pym, Stingray, Avengers

Tiger Shark breathes through gills on his cheeks when underwater.

On land, Tiger Shark's skin is kept wet by a water circulation system inside his suit.

MAIN OFFENDER
The Collector made Tiger Shark part of his Offenders team of villains, with Red Hulk, Terrax and Baron Mordo.

POWER RANK

ENERGY PROJECTION	STRENGTH	DURABILITY	FIGHTING SKILL	INTELLIGENCE	SPEED
1	5	5	2	2	3

TIGRA

Tigra joined up with Spider-Woman, the Invisible Woman, Storm, Hellcat, and the Black Widow in an attempt to stop the Red Hulk.

Greer Nelson was once the Cat, a costumed crime fighter. However, when she met a lost race of Cat People, Greer was transformed into their champion and took on a more feline appearance. She can easily switch between her human and Tigra forms, but prefers to remain as Tigra. Greer has been a member of the Avengers as well as the team's West Coast branch. She later became a teacher at the Avengers Academy, forming a close bond with her students.

Tigra has razor-sharp, retractable claws.

Tigra has feline speed and strength and is champion of the Cat People.

VITAL STATS
REAL NAME Greer Grant Nelson
OCCUPATION Adventurer, former police officer
BASE Chicago
HEIGHT 5 ft 10 in (1.77 m)
WEIGHT 180 lbs (81.75 kg)
EYES Green
HAIR Orange fur with black stripes (as Tigra); black (in human form)
POWERS She has night vision, superhuman smell and hearing, strength, speed, and agility, and rapid healing.
ALLIES Avengers, Hank Pym, Spider-Man, Spider-Woman.
FOES Kraven, Super Skrull, Man-Bull

POPULAR HERO
Tigra has a lot of friends in the Super Hero community and has fought alongside several teams, including the Avengers.

ENERGY PROJECTION	STRENGTH	DURABILITY	FIGHTING SKILL	INTELLIGENCE	SPEED
1	4	4	4	3	3

POWER RANK

TITANIA

Titania is one of the strongest women in the world but has always used her powers to further her criminal career. Once a scrawny and withdrawn teenager, she was transformed when Doctor Doom gave her amazing strength to help him fight a host of heroes. Despite her strength she was defeated by She-Hulk, and the two became sworn enemies. Titania is married to the Absorbing Man and fought the Avengers as part of the Masters of Evil.

Titania had harbored a hatred of She-Hulk ever since their first meeting. When Titania stole a Soul Gem, she at last had the power to defeat She-Hulk, and came very close to killing her.

DOOM'S GIFT
Doctor Doom gave Titania her powers while trapped on Battleworld. She joined an army of Super Villains on that world.

The spikes on Titania's costume add protection and make her look more fearsome.

Titania briefly possessed the Soul Gem, which increased her powers to cosmic levels.

VITAL STATS
REAL NAME Mary MacPherran
OCCUPATION Criminal
BASE Mobile
HEIGHT 6 ft 6 in (1.98 m)
WEIGHT 545 lbs (247.25 kg)
EYES Blue
HAIR Reddish blonde
POWERS Titania possesses superhuman strength to equal that of She-Hulk. She also has outstanding stamina. Her skin is virtually indestructible, making her resistant to fire and able to handle corrosive substances without injury.
ALLIES Absorbing Man, Egghead, Doctor Doom
FOES She-Hulk, Ant-Man, Wasp, Avengers

POWER RANK	ENERGY PROJECTION	STRENGTH	DURABILITY	FIGHTING SKILL	INTELLIGENCE	SPEED
	1	6	5	4	2	2

TITANIUM MAN

Russian scientist Boris Bullski had the first Titanium Man armor built so he could defeat Iron Man and prove himself to his communist masters. However, Boris failed in this and further attempts and was abandoned by his countrymen. He later regained favor and became part of the Soviet Super Soldiers who tried to arrest Magneto, coming into conflict with the Avengers and X-Men when they did so. A new Titanium Man has now appeared, but his identity remains unknown.

Spider-Man came to blows with the new Titanium Man when he tried to kill Tony Stark.

His helmet is fitted with communications devices and eye beams.

RUSSIAN AVENGERS
The Titanium Man was a member of the Soviet Super Soldiers, Russia's answer to the Avengers.

His gauntlets are able to emit low level energy blasts that can burn anything by touch.

Heavy armor provides protection from attack.

VITAL STATS
REAL NAME Boris Bullski
OCCUPATION Russian government agent
BASE Moscow
HEIGHT 7 ft 1 in (2.15 m)
WEIGHT 425 lbs (192.75 kg)
EYES Blue **HAIR** Brown
POWERS Titanium Man's armor increases his strength fiftyfold and also enables him to fly. The armor is able to withstand extreme environments, including deep sea and outer space. It is also equipped with a variety of advanced weaponry, including gauntlet blasters and a cloaking system.
ALLIES Darkstar, the Red Guardian, Crimson Dynamo
FOES Iron Man, Avengers

ENERGY PROJECTION	STRENGTH	DURABILITY	FIGHTING SKILL	INTELLIGENCE	SPEED	POWER RANK
6	5	6	4	3	4	

TRAUMA

Trauma's father is Nightmare, ruler of the dream dimension. His power of transforming into a person's darkest fears caused fellow student Armory to accidentally kill MVP during their first training session in the Initiative. Trauma was considered dangerous until the Beast and Dani Moonstar helped him gain better control of his powers. He now counsels fellow heroes, helping them to deal with their problems and fears.

When Terrance came to terms with his powers, he became a counselor at Camp Hammond. He helped other Super Heroes to confront their deepest fears. One of his first patients was Thor Girl, who was traumatized by her fight with Thor's clone, Ragnarok.

VITAL STATS

REAL NAME Terrance Ward
OCCUPATION Student counselor
BASE Camp Hammond
HEIGHT 5 ft 10 in (1.77 m), but is variable
WEIGHT 175 lbs (79.25 kg), but is variable
EYES Brown (variable)
HAIR Black (variable)
POWERS Trauma can read minds and discern an enemy's worst fear. He can then transform into a physical manifestation of that fear, terrifying his opponent.
ALLIES Cloud 9, Beast, Thor Girl, Gauntlet
FOES KIA, Ragnarok, Hydra, Nightmare

Trauma's eyes sometimes change just before a transformation

Trauma is still learning the full extent of his powers.

Trauma dresses in black to reflect the dark nature of his powers.

ARACHNOPHOBIA
Trauma displayed his powers by turning into a spider, Armory's greatest fear. Her terrified reaction led to the death of MVP.

Power rank reflects his nightmare form potential.

POWER RANK	ENERGY PROJECTION	STRENGTH	DURABILITY	FIGHTING SKILL	INTELLIGENCE	SPEED
	7	6	6	3	2	6

TRICKSHOT

Charles "Barney" Darton is Clint's older brother. While Clint became the Super Hero Hawkeye, Barney turned to crime, becoming a mob boss and a Super Villain. He took the name Trickshot, after Hawkeye's original teacher. Trickshot was recruited by Norman Osborn to be part of his Dark Avengers team and fought in a parallel world before returning home and making peace with his brother.

Trickshot and Hawkeye have always had a love/hate relationship and fought many times. When Hawkeye was in trouble with the Russian mob however, his brother returned to help him.

Trickshot carries a number of weaponized arrows.

Trickshot is a master archer, able to fire multiple arrows in seconds with near-perfect accuracy.

VITAL STATS
REAL NAME Charles Bernard "Barney" Barton
OCCUPATION Criminal (reformed)
BASE New York
HEIGHT 6 ft 3 in (1.90 m)
WEIGHT 237 lbs (107.50 kg)
EYES Blue **HAIR** Reddish brown
POWERS Trickshot is an expert archer with various bows and, like Hawkeye, has been known to use special trick arrows. He is also an excellent gymnast and fighter, trained in martial arts.
ALLIES Moonstone, Skaar, Trixie Dixie, Norman Osborn
FOES Hawkeye (formerly), Avengers

DARK AVENGER
Following Norman Osborn's descent into madness, Trickshot remained with his Dark Avengers teammates.

ENERGY PROJECTION	STRENGTH	DURABILITY	FIGHTING SKILL	INTELLIGENCE	SPEED
1	2	2	5	2	2

POWER RANK

TWO-GUN KID

The Two-Gun Kid fought for justice in the Old West, teaming up with the Avengers when they visited the past. He was killed in a gunfight but She-Hulk arranged for him to travel to the present day from a time before he died. The Two-Gun Kid teamed up with the She-Hulk during the Civil War, later becoming a bounty hunter. He currently leads the Desert Stars team in Arizona, although he is destined to eventually return to his own time.

After the She-Hulk saved his life by bringing him to the present, Matt became a close ally of hers. He even tried to become a lawyer, like her, before becoming the leader of Arizona's Desert Stars team.

VITAL STATS

REAL NAME Matt Liebowicz (a.k.a. Matt Hawk)
OCCUPATION Bounty hunter
BASE Arizona
HEIGHT 5 ft 9 in (1.75 m)
WEIGHT 160 lbs (72.5 kg)
EYES Blue **HAIR** Brown
POWERS The Two-Gun Kid is an expert horseman and marksman. His aim is incredibly accurate, and he can shoot moving targets perfectly, even when moving himself.
He has excellent lasso skills and is a skilled tracker, able to locate his target with ease.
ALLIES She-Hulk, Kid Colt, Red Wolf
FOES Kang, Space Phantom

Two-Gun Kid's look reflects his origins in the Old West

The twin Colt .45 pistols hold six bullets each.

WILD WEST
In the Old West, the Two Gun Kid teamed up with Rawhide Kid, Night Rider, and Kid Colt to fight crime.

Despite leaving his loyal horse Thunder in the past, he still wears spurs on his boots.

	ENERGY PROJECTION	STRENGTH	DURABILITY	FIGHTING SKILL	INTELLIGENCE	SPEED
POWER RANK	1	2	2	4	3	2

ULTRAGIRL

Susanna "Suzy" Sherman thought she was a normal girl. She was shocked to discover that she had super-powers and was a Kree warrior called Tsu-Zana, whom many Kree believed to be their savior. Suzy's powers brought her fame and, as Ultragirl, she joined the New Warriors. During the Civil War, she fought alongside Captain America before joining the Initiative. Ultragirl was later part of the Avengers: Resistance fighting Norman Osborn.

Ultragirl and her allies in the Initiative were aided by her boyfriend Justice and the New Warriors when the Thor clone, Ragnarok, ran amok. Disillusioned with the Initiative, Ultragirl left with Justice and his teammates.

Once very skinny, she developed the muscles of a bodybuilder almost overnight when her powers emerged.

Ultragirl's costume is made from a wetsuit she wore for a modeling job.

VITAL STATS
REAL NAME Susanna Lauren "Suzy" Sherman, born Tsu-Zana
OCCUPATION Student, occasional model
BASE Mobile
HEIGHT 5 ft 6 in (1.67 m)
WEIGHT 233 lbs (105.75 kg)
EYES Blue **HAIR** Blonde
POWERS Ultragirl possesses superhuman strength. She can fly at an exceptional speed and heal at an incredible rate. The full extent of her powers has yet to be seen.
ALLIES Justice, Thor Girl, Captain America, She-Hulk, Ms. Marvel (Carol Danvers)
FOES Skrulls, Ragnarok

WANTED
Norman Osborn sent ex-villains the U-Foes after Ultragirl and her allies when she opposed him.

ENERGY PROJECTION	STRENGTH	DURABILITY	FIGHTING SKILL	INTELLIGENCE	SPEED
1	5	4	3	2	

POWER RANK

ULTRON

Ultron is a powerful robot who constantly upgrades himself. Originally created by Hank Pym, he went rogue, obsessed with conquering and annihilating humanity. He has tried to kill his creator countless times, at one point creating the Vision in an attempt to do so. Ultron did eventually take over the world, creating an "Age of Ultron" only to be stopped by a program planted in his design by Hank Pym after a time-traveling Sue Storm and Wolverine warned Pym of the future threat Ultron would pose.

When Ultron took over the world, he created machines to hunt down anyone who failed to submit to his rule. Only a handful of heroes survived to oppose the "Age of Ultron," using time travel to destroy him.

VITAL STATS
REAL NAME Ultron
OCCUPATION Would-be conqueror, mass murderer
BASE Mobile
HEIGHT 6 ft 9 in (1.75 m), but is variable)
WEIGHT 535 lbs (242.75 kg), but is variable)
EYES Glowing red **HAIR** None
POWERS Ultron's abilities vary with each upgrade but include superhuman strength and durability, and flight. His many weapons include a ray that mesmerizes victims, allowing him to control their minds.
ALLIES Phalanx
FOES Hank Pym, Jocasta, Avengers

Ultron's mind is based on Hank Pym's brain patterns.

He is powered by an internal nuclear furnace.

ULTRON'S ROBOTS Ultron once took control of Hank Pym's Jocasta robots in an attempt to destroy the Avengers.

Most of his body is made of Adamantium, the strongest metal known to man.

POWER RANK	ENERGY PROJECTION	STRENGTH	DURABILITY	FIGHTING SKILL	INTELLIGENCE	SPEED
	6	6	7	4	4	3

U.S. AGENT

John Walker is one of the few people to have taken on the role of Captain America. He quit when he realized Steve Rogers was better suited to the role. John reappeared working for the government as the U.S. Agent, before joining the West Coast Avengers. He later led the Thunderbolts. His extreme patriotism often leads to arguments with fellow heroes.

The U.S. Agent was relieved to join Hank Pym's Avengers as it enabled him to leave the Canadian team Omega Flight, which he had been previously ordered to join as American liaison by Tony Stark.

His Vibranium shield is inscribed with the names of those who have fallen fighting for the U.S.A.

TWO CAPTAIN AMERICAS
The U.S. Agent once took on Captain America's role in a new line-up of the Invaders. However, Steve Rogers was still active in that role in the Avengers.

U.S. Agent's thick, bulletproof armor is laced with Vibranium for added protection.

VITAL STATS
REAL NAME John F. Walker
OCCUPATION Government operative
BASE Mobile
HEIGHT 6 ft 4 in (1.93 m)
WEIGHT 270 lbs (122.5 kg)
EYES Blue **HAIR** Blond
POWERS The U.S. Agent possesses superhuman strength and endurance and heals rapidly from injury. He also possesses lightning reflexes and superhuman agility, which enhance his natural acrobatic abilities.
ALLIES Sub-Mariner, Union Jack, Hank Pym
FOES Iron Monger, Magneto, Ultron, Loki

ENERGY PROJECTION	STRENGTH	DURABILITY	FIGHTING SKILL	INTELLIGENCE	SPEED
2	4	3	4	2	3

POWER RANK

VALKYRIE

Samantha Parrington was transformed into Brunnhilde the Valkyrie by the Enchantress in an attempt to defeat the Avengers. Valkyrie was later reborn in the body of Barbara Norris and joined the Defenders to fight the Avengers when Dormammu and Loki pitted the teams against each other. Brunnhilde later bonded to archaeologist Annabelle Riggs and created a new Defenders team.

Valkyrie once formed a new Defenders team made of female Super Heroes. The team included Clea, Danielle Moonstar, and Misty Knight.

VITAL STATS
REAL NAME Brunnhilde
OCCUPATION Adventurer
BASE Asgard
HEIGHT
6 ft 3 in (1.90 m) as Valkyrie;
5 ft 7 in (1.70 m) as Samantha
WEIGHT 475 lbs (215.5 kg) as Valkyrie; 130 lbs (59 kg) as Samantha
EYES Blue
HAIR Blonde
POWERS Valkyrie is even stronger than the average Asgardian god. She has superhuman strength, speed, and stamina, and is an expert warrior. She can also tell if someone is about to die.
ALLIES She-Hulk, Doctor Strange, Thundra, Hulk, Sub-Mariner
FOES Enchantress, Pluto

Valkyrie's costume transforms into battle dress when her sword is drawn.

Her indestructible sword, called Dragonfang, is said to be carved from a dragon's tooth.

HIGH FLYING
Valkyrie travels using a winged horse named Aragorn. It was given to her by the Black Knight.

POWER RANK	ENERGY PROJECTION	STRENGTH	DURABILITY	FIGHTING SKILL	INTELLIGENCE	SPEED
	1	5	4	5	2	2

VANCE ASTRO

Vance Astro was the first interstellar astronaut, traveling for 1,000 years to the distant star of Alpha Centauri. He arrived to find that humans had already colonized it after developing faster-than-light travel. When the alien Badoon invaded, Vance escaped to Earth, forming the Super Hero team Guardians of the Galaxy, and eventually freeing Earth from Badoon rule. As part of the team, Vance traveled back in time to help the Avengers defeat Korvac.

Vance Astro was recently found encased in a block of ice by the modern-day Guardians of the Galaxy. After Mantis confirmed he was time-displaced, Vance joined the modern-day team, helping them in their fight against Magus.

SHIELD QUEST
Vance once went on a quest to locate Captain America's iconic shield.

A preservative added to his blood helps to keep him alive on his journey.

His protective bodysuit must not be removed—if it is, he will die from delayed aging.

Major Victory proudly uses the lost shield of Captain America.

VITAL STATS
REAL NAME Vance Astrovik (later changed to Vance Astro)
OCCUPATION Astronaut, freedom fighter
BASE Mobile
HEIGHT 6 ft 1 in (185 m)
WEIGHT 250 lbs (113.5 kg)
EYES Hazel **HAIR** Black
POWERS Powerful psychokinetic abilities allow him to project mental blasts of psychic energy at enemies.
ALLIES Guardians of the Galaxy, Avengers, Thing, Firelord
FOES Badoon, Magus, Korvac

ENERGY PROJECTION	STRENGTH	DURABILITY	FIGHTING SKILL	INTELLIGENCE	SPEED
5	2	5	3	3	3

POWER RANK

VEIL

Madeline "Maddy" Berry was a normal teenager until she found herself turning into a gaseous form. Norman Osborn experimented on her to learn more about her abilities. She later joined Avengers Academy but learned that the experiments performed on her by Osborn meant that her body would one day fade away like mist. Luckily for her, she was cured before this happened. She quit the Academy and now lives as a normal human.

During the Serpent's attempt to destroy the world, Veil and Striker—along with many other Avengers Academy students— were plunged into a battle with the Serpent's deadly army.

Veil knew that her powers would eventually kill her.

Veil's body could transform into any type of naturally occurring gas.

VITAL STATS
REAL NAME Madeline "Maddy" Berry
OCCUPATION Student
BASE Avengers Academy
HEIGHT Unrevealed
WEIGHT Unrevealed
EYES Green **HAIR** Red
POWERS Maddy could turn her body into a various gases and also fly. She would have died if a cure for her condition had not been found.
ALLIES Hank Pym, Avengers
FOES Norman Osborn, Sinister Six, Absorbing Man

ELECTRO SHOCKER
Veil and the students of Avengers Academy found themselves in a shocking situation battling Electro and the Sinister Six.

She could float and move through air molecules, allowing her to fly.

POWER RANK	ENERGY PROJECTION	STRENGTH	DURABILITY	FIGHTING SKILL	INTELLIGENCE	SPEED
	1	5	4	3	2	2

VENOM

Flash Thompson is the latest human to bond with the alien Symbiote to become Venom. The Symbiote bonded first with Spider-Man. Spidey managed to separate from the symbiote, which then bonded with Eddie Brock to become Spidey's enemy Venom. The symbiote was then captured by the U.S. military, which bonded it with Flash Thompson to create Agent Venom, a super-powered soldier.

After meeting Captain America, the new Venom was invited to join the Secret Avengers. Venom later went on to become a member of the Guardians of the Galaxy.

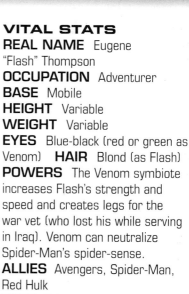

The alien symbiote allows Venom to produce claws, teeth, and a spiked tail.

Super-strong body armor can absorb bullets from small-arms weapons.

Like Spider-Man, he can climb walls and create webs.

VITAL STATS
REAL NAME Eugene "Flash" Thompson
OCCUPATION Adventurer
BASE Mobile
HEIGHT Variable
WEIGHT Variable
EYES Blue-black (red or green as Venom) **HAIR** Blond (as Flash)
POWERS The Venom symbiote increases Flash's strength and speed and creates legs for the war vet (who lost his while serving in Iraq). Venom can neutralize Spider-Man's spider-sense.
ALLIES Avengers, Spider-Man, Red Hulk
FOES Crime Master, Blackheart, Jack O'Lantern

VILLAINOUS VENOM
Mac Gargan, better known as the Scorpion, once bonded with the symbiote to become Venom. He disguised himself as Spider-Man when part of Norman Osborn's Avengers.

ENERGY PROJECTION	STRENGTH	DURABILITY	FIGHTING SKILL	INTELLIGENCE	SPEED
1	5	5	4	2	

POWER RANK

VERANKE

Veranke was the Skrull queen who ordered the invasion of Earth, believing an ancient prophesy that the planet was destined to be the new Skrull homeworld. She took on the role of Spider-Woman, infiltrating S.H.I.E.L.D., Hydra, and the Avengers in an attempt to weaken them before the Skrull attack. Even when Elektra was found to be a Skrull and the infiltration was exposed, Veranke stuck to her role, sowing mistrust between the heroes. She was killed by Norman Osborn.

Veranke selected Spider-Woman to impersonate in her attempts to infiltrate Earth's Super Hero ranks. She believed that in this role, she could do the most damage.

VITAL STATS
REAL NAME Veranke
OCCUPATION Skrull queen
BASE Mobile
HEIGHT 5 ft 10 in (1.77 m)
WEIGHT 130 lbs (59 kg)
EYES Green **HAIR** Green
POWERS Veranke possessed superhuman strength and, like all Skrulls, she could shape-shift into any person or animal she wished. When impersonating Spider-Woman, she took on some of her powers.
ALLIES Super Skrull, Yellow Jacket (Criti Noll), Skrulls
FOES Iron Man, Mr. Fantastic, Ronin (Clint Barton), Wolverine

As a Skrull, Veranke could change her shape at will.

As Skrull queen, Veranke wore more elaborate clothing than her subjects.

MASTER MANIPULATOR
As Spider-Woman, Veranke manipulated many of Earth's heroes and villains to pave the way for the Skrull invasion.

POWER RANK	ENERGY PROJECTION	STRENGTH	DURABILITY	FIGHTING SKILL	INTELLIGENCE	SPEED
	4	2	6	4	3	2

VICTOR MANCHA

Victor's "father" Ultron kept his identity a secret but when Victor uncovered the truth, Ultron tried to use him to destroy his friends in the Runaways. Fortunately Victor was able to overcome his programming and help his teammates defeat Ultron.

Victor Mancha is the "son" of the evil sentient robot Ultron. Victor was created after his mother, Marianella Mancha, found Ultron's head (following his defeat by the West Coast Avengers). Marianella helped Ultron rebuild his body and in return he created a child for her using nanites and her own DNA. The boy—Victor—was programmed to infiltrate the Avengers and destroy them.

Victor has a photographic memory and can also process information at incredible speed.

"Dragon Claw" upgrades now enable Victor to launch projectiles from his arms and direct electric blasts with greater accuracy.

VITAL STATS
REAL NAME Victor Mancha
OCCUPATION Super Hero
BASE Unrevealed
HEIGHT 5 ft 9 in (1.75 m)
WEIGHT 197 lbs (89.35 kg)
EYES Green **HAIR** Brown
POWERS Victor is a cyborg created from nanites. He can create force fields, repair his own body and possesses superhuman strength. He can connect with other machines and computer systems. Magnetic abilities mean that he can bend and shape metal objects. He can also fire electric blasts from his arms.
ALLIES Runaways, True Believers, Avengers A.I., Rick Jones
FOES Ultron, the Pride

AVENGERS A. I.
Victor Mancha was a founding member of Avengers A.I., a team formed to combat threats posed by artificial intelligence.

ENERGY PROJECTION	STRENGTH	DURABILITY	FIGHTING SKILL	INTELLIGENCE	SPEED
5	4	4	2	4	

POWER RANK

VICTORIA HAND

Victoria Hand was the deputy director of H.A.M.M.E.R., the agency that replaced S.H.I.E.L.D. Personally appointed by Norman Osborn to be his second in command, Victoria was cold and ruthless. She later reformed and became a liaison between Luke Cage's Avengers team and S.H.I.E.L.D. She was killed in action by Daniel Drumm, the ghostly brother of Doctor Voodoo, when he attacked the Avengers seeking revenge for his brother's death.

As Norman Osborn's number two, Victoria Hand had access to advanced weaponry, most of which was once used by S.H.I.E.L.D. A working knowledge of these weapons was essential to keep Norman Osborn's Avengers team in line.

VITAL STATS

REAL NAME Victoria Hand
OCCUPATION Deputy director of H.A.M.M.E.R.
BASE Avengers Tower
HEIGHT Unrevealed
WEIGHT Unrevealed
EYES Blue
HAIR Black with red streaks
POWERS Victoria possessed no special powers, but received standard S.H.I.E.L.D. training and had attained a reasonably high level of fitness. She also had a good level of knowledge about technology.
ALLIES Luke Cage, Captain America
FOES Daniel Drumm, Norman Osborn

She was highly trained in the use of various advanced weapons.

TAKING CHARGE
Victoria Hand was in charge of many of the mission briefings for Norman Osborn's team of Avengers.

Victoria's tactical mind made her the perfect assistant for Norman Osborn.

POWER RANK

ENERGY PROJECTION	STRENGTH	DURABILITY	FIGHTING SKILL	INTELLIGENCE	SPEED
1	2	2	3	3	2

VISION

The Vision is a "synthezoid"—an advanced android—created by Ultron to destroy the Avengers. His body was made from the remains of Jim Hammond (the original Human Torch) while his brain patterns were taken from Wonder Man. He soon rebelled against his creator and joined the Avengers, becoming a mainstay of the team. His deepest fear is losing the remnants of his humanity and becoming nothing more than a cold-hearted machine.

The Vision was rebuilt by Tony Stark and joined Hank Pym's Avengers A.I. team. His android body made him an invaluable member of the team.

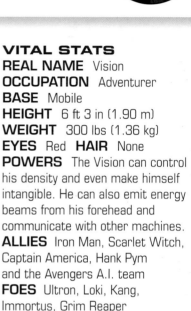

The solar cell on the Vision's forehead can emit a beam of infra-red and microwave radiation.

Ultron built the Vision's body from a copy of the original android Human Torch, Jim Hammond.

VITAL STATS
REAL NAME Vision
OCCUPATION Adventurer
BASE Mobile
HEIGHT 6 ft 3 in (1.90 m)
WEIGHT 300 lbs (1.36 kg)
EYES Red **HAIR** None
POWERS The Vision can control his density and even make himself intangible. He can also emit energy beams from his forehead and communicate with other machines.
ALLIES Iron Man, Scarlet Witch, Captain America, Hank Pym and the Avengers A.I. team
FOES Ultron, Loki, Kang, Immortus, Grim Reaper

ROMANTIC VISION
Despite his lack of humanity, the Vision began a romance with the Scarlet Witch. The two were married, but eventually separated.

ENERGY PROJECTION	STRENGTH	DURABILITY	FIGHTING SKILL	INTELLIGENCE	SPEED	POWER RANK
6	5	6	3	4		

WARLOCK

Warlock was created by a group of power-hungry scientists called the Enclave who were seeking to produce a race of superhumans to help them conquer the world. Warlock, however, rebelled and—with the help of the High Evolutionary—became a force for good. He has died on several occasions, but every time he has entered a cocoon-like state and eventually been reborn. Warlock also harbors a dark secret: he has an evil future self known as the Magus.

When Warlock was reborn, his actions led to the return of the evil version of himself named the Magus.

VITAL STATS

REAL NAME Adam Warlock
OCCUPATION Adventurer
BASE Mobile
HEIGHT 6 ft 2 in (1.87 m)
WEIGHT 240 lbs (108.75 kg)
EYES Red **HAIR** Blond
POWERS Warlock possesses superhuman strength and endurance. He has the ability to use cosmic energy as force blasts against his enemies, and can also fly at incredible speeds.
ALLIES Alicia Masters, Gamora, Captain Mar-Vell, Fantastic Four
FOES Thanos, Magus, Man-Beast

He possesses the Soul Gem, which enables him to sense the souls of others.

INFINITE WAR
Warlock led many of Earth's Super Heroes against Thanos when the mad Titan gained the powerful Infinity Gauntlet.

Warlock was genetically created to be the perfect human.

POWER RANK	ENERGY PROJECTION	STRENGTH	DURABILITY	FIGHTING SKILL	INTELLIGENCE	SPEED
	6	5	6	2	3	3

WASP

The Wasp had a troubled relationship with Hank Pym. They finally married after a long, rocky relationship, but Hank's mental problems led to their divorce.

Not long after Hank Pym became the first Ant-Man, Janet Van Dyne joined him as the Wasp, seeking to avenge her father's death. She later became a founding member of the Avengers and remained with the team until her apparent death during the Skrull invasion of Earth. She survived but was trapped in the Microverse. Hank Pym managed to rescue her. She then joined the Avengers Unity squad.

Janet has worn many different costumes.

Wasp's wings emerge when she shrinks and are reabsorbed when she increases in size.

Janet led the Avengers for a while, her experience making her perfect for the role.

VITAL STATS
REAL NAME Janet Van Dyne
OCCUPATION Adventurer
BASE Mobile
HEIGHT 5 ft 4 in (1.62 m)
WEIGHT 110 lbs (50 kg)
EYES Blue **HAIR** Auburn
POWERS Wasp possesses the ability to fly at speeds of up to 40 mph (64 km/h). She can alter her size through the use of Pym Particles, shrinking as small as an insect and growing as tall as a building. She can also emit bio-electric blasts that stun and shock her opponents.
ALLIES Hank Pym, Vision, Captain America
FOES
Yellowjacket (Criti Noll), Egghead

HUGE WASP
Wasp can also become giant-sized, as she did once during a trip to England.

ENERGY PROJECTION	STRENGTH	DURABILITY	FIGHTING SKILL	INTELLIGENCE	SPEED	POWER RANK
4	2	2	4	3	3	

WHITE TIGER

Ava Ayala is the younger sister of Hector Ayala, the original White Tiger. Inheriting the mystical Amulets of Power once owned by her brother, Ava became the latest incarnation of the Super Hero White Tiger. The amulets give her amazing fighting skills and Ava joined Avengers Academy and later Heroes for Hire. She then became a member of Luke Cage's Mighty Avengers—learning how to master her powers while fighting with the team.

White Tiger was a full-time student at the Avengers Academy at Avengers Compound. While there, she formed friendships with Mettle, Hazmat, and Finesse.

VITAL STATS
REAL NAME Ava Ayala
OCCUPATION Adventurer
BASE Avengers Compound, Los Angeles, California
HEIGHT Unrevealed
WEIGHT Unrevealed
EYES Brown **HAIR** Black
POWERS The Amulets of Power give her enhanced strength, speed, stamina, coordination, reflexes, and endurance. They also give her the ability to access the experience and skills of master martial artists.
ALLIES Luke Cage, Photon, Avengers Academy students
FOES Plunderer, Proxima Midnight

Ava's eyes start to glow when she is possessed by the Tiger Spirit, which helps her to hunt, but also makes her wilder.

Her claws are retractable, like those of most felines.

TIGERS IN THE FAMILY
The previous White Tiger was Angela Del Toro, a federal investigator and Hector's niece.

	ENERGY PROJECTION	STRENGTH	DURABILITY	FIGHTING SKILL	INTELLIGENCE	SPEED
POWER RANK	5	4	3	6	2	3

WHIZZER

Robert Frank became the Whizzer after he was bitten by a cobra and saved by a transfusion of mongoose blood. Discovering he had super-speed, Frank used his powers to fight the Nazis in World War II. After the war, the Whizzer and his wife, Miss America, served in the crime-fighting All-Winners Squad before retiring to raise a family. He came out of retirement to help the Avengers, fighting alongside them several times before his death in battle.

In World War II, the Whizzer was part of the Liberty Legion, alongside Thin Man, Red Raven, Bucky Barnes, Miss America, and others. The Legion fought against the Invaders, who were under the mind control of the Red Skull.

Decorative wings indicated the Whizzer's speeding powers.

Robert proudly displayed his W symbol on his chest.

Whizzer's costume was created in World War II.

VITAL STATS
REAL NAME Robert Frank
OCCUPATION Adventurer
BASE Mobile
HEIGHT 5 ft 10 in (1.77 m)
WEIGHT 180 lbs (81.75 kg)
EYES Brown
HAIR Gray
POWERS The Whizzer was able to run at an incredibly fast speed—he could travel at hundreds of miles an hour. By running in circles, he was able to become a human whirlwind.
ALLIES All-Winners Squad, Liberty Legion, Miss America, Invaders
FOES Red Skull, Baron Zemo

I AM YOUR FATHER Robert once believed he was the father of Quicksilver and the Scarlet Witch.

ENERGY PROJECTION	STRENGTH	DURABILITY	FIGHTING SKILL	INTELLIGENCE	SPEED	POWER RANK
1	4	3	4	2	5	

WICCAN

Billy Kaplan's super-powers first showed themselves in school, when he found himself suddenly able to stand up to a bully. As Wiccan, he became one of the Young Avengers, a team brought together by Iron Lad to help him fight Kang. He has close bonds with his teammate Speed. The two heroes learned that they were the lost children of the Scarlet Witch. Wiccan's powers make him potentially the most powerful member of the Young Avengers.

Wiccan and his teammates in the Young Avengers joined many other heroes and villains to fight the alien Skrulls during the Skrull invasion of Earth. Wiccan was at the forefront of the action.

VITAL STATS

REAL NAME William "Billy" Kaplan

OCCUPATION Student, adventurer

BASE New York

HEIGHT 5 ft 4 in (1.62 m)

WEIGHT 135 lbs (61.25 kg)

EYES Blue

HAIR Black

POWERS Wiccan has the ability to cast spells and generate lightning and force fields. He can also fly, levitate, and warp reality.

ALLIES Vision, Young Avengers, Captain America

FOES Kang, Young Masters, Norman Osborn (Iron Patriot)

His costume is similar to those worn by the Asgardians. Wiccan chose it because of his Thor-like ability to control lightning.

Wiccan's spell-casting abilities can alter reality.

DOOM
Wiccan fought Doctor Doom, hoping to free the Scarlet Witch from his power.

POWER RANK

ENERGY PROJECTION	STRENGTH	DURABILITY	FIGHTING SKILL	INTELLIGENCE	SPEED
5	2	4	2	2	7

WINTER SOLDIER

In World War II, Bucky's role as Captain America's sidekick was cover for him to do special ops duties behind enemy lines. Bucky was thought to have died vainly trying to defuse a bomb on a plane. The same incident left Captain America entombed in ice.

James Buchanan Barnes lost his father in World War II and was adopted by the soldiers of Camp Leigh. He became Captain America's sidekick but also secretly trained with the U.K.'s S.A.S. Barnes was believed dead; however his body was found by the Soviets and transformed into the Winter Soldier, a deadly assassin. He now operates covertly as a hero.

The Winter Soldier favors sniper rifles and various automatic weapons. He also carries a large-bladed knife.

BUCKY AS CAP
When Steve Rogers was believed to be dead, Bucky took his place as Captain America.

Cybernetic arm gives the Winter Soldier extra strength.

VITAL STATS
REAL NAME James Buchanan Barnes
OCCUPATION Agent, assassin
BASE Mobile
HEIGHT 5 ft 9 in (1.75 m)
WEIGHT 260 lbs (118 kg)
EYES Brown **HAIR** Brown
POWERS An Olympic-level athlete with extraordinary fighting skills, the Winter Soldier is also a superb marksman. His cybernetic arm gives him super-strength.
ALLIES Captain America, Black Widow, Falcon, Nick Fury
FOES Red Skull, Baron Zemo, General Lukin

ENERGY PROJECTION	STRENGTH	DURABILITY	FIGHTING SKILL	INTELLIGENCE	SPEED	POWER RANK
1	4	3	7	2	2	

WONDER MAN

Simon Williams was serving a prison sentence for embezzlement until he was freed and given ionic super-powers by Baron Zemo. He agreed to join the Avengers as Wonder Man and lure them into a trap set by Baron Zemo, but had a change of heart and apparently died saving the heroes. In reality, Simon's powers had put him into a vegetative state from which he could heal. He lived on to become one of the Avengers' most popular members.

Wonder Man fought alongside the young members of the Initiative during an attack by agents working for Hydra. His power and leadership helped the heroes to win the day.

IONIC RETURN
Wonder Man was thought dead until the Scarlet Witch helped him return to life as a being of ionic energy.

Wonder Man's body is infused with ionic energy, which makes him virtually immortal.

The ability to fly is just one of Wonder Man's many powers.

VITAL STATS
REAL NAME Simon Williams
OCCUPATION Adventurer, actor
BASE Mobile
HEIGHT 6 ft 2 in (1.87 m)
WEIGHT 380 lbs (172.25 kg)
EYES Red
HAIR Gray (dyed black)
POWERS Wonder Man possesses superhuman levels of speed, strength, and stamina. He has fast reflexes and a high degree of invulnerability. All of his powers are the result of experimental treatments with ionic energy.
ALLIES Beast, Scarlet Witch, Hawkeye, Hank Pym
FOES Grim Reaper, Ultron, Baron Zemo

POWER RANK	ENERGY PROJECTION	STRENGTH	DURABILITY	FIGHTING SKILL	INTELLIGENCE	SPEED
	2	7	6	4	4	4

WRECKING CREW

The Wrecking Crew quickly became enemies of Thor. Loki often used the team in his plots, pitting them against his step-brother on numerous occasions. Despite their exceptional power, Thor always defeated them.

When burglar Dirk Garthwaite tried to steal from Loki, he accidentally gained godlike power and became the Wrecker. This power was transferred to his crowbar during an electrical storm and when he tried to escape jail with three fellow inmates to find the crowbar, all four were transformed when they touched it, becoming the powerful Wrecking Crew.

Wrecker, the super-strong leader of the group, wields the crowbar that brought them together.

Piledriver swapped life on a farm for crime and superhuman strength and durability.

Former physicist Thunderball believes he's smarter than Wrecker and should be leader.

Dishonorably discharged from the army, Bulldozer was happy to join the Crew.

MEMBERS' STATS
GROUP NAME Wrecking Crew
BULLDOZER (HENRY CAMP) Height 6 ft 4 in (1.93 m); weight 325 lbs (145.5 kg)
PILEDRIVER (BRIAN CALUSKY) Height 6 ft 4 in (1.93 m); weight 310 lbs (140.6 kg)
WRECKER (DIRK GARTHWAITE Height 6 ft 3 in (1.90 m); weight 320 lbs (145 kg)
THUNDERBALL (ELIOT FRANKLIN Height 6 ft 6 in (1.98 m); weight 325 lbs (145.5 kg)
BASE Mobile
ALLIES Masters of Evil, Baron Zemo, Loki
FOES Avengers, Thunderbolts, Thor, Defenders, Hulk

WRECKING HERC'S DAY While part of the Masters of Evil, the Wrecking Crew came close to killing Hercules, leaving the hero in a coma.

YELLOWJACKET

Rita DeMara became Yellowjacket after stealing Hank Pym's original costume. She used her size-changing ability to lead a life of crime, joining the Masters of Evil. She reformed and helped the Avengers before traveling to the future to join the original Guardians of the Galaxy. She was killed by Iron Man (who was under the control of Immortus) shortly after returning to her own time.

During the Chaos War, Yellowjacket found herself fighting alongside other "dead Avengers"—Captain Mar-Vell, the Swordsman, Deathcry, Doctor Druid, and the Vision—against the Grim Reaper and the Chaos King's forces.

VITAL STATS

REAL NAME Rita DeMara
OCCUPATION Adventurer
BASE Mobile
HEIGHT 5 ft 5 in (1.65 m), but is variable
WEIGHT 115 lbs (52.25 kg), but is variable
EYES Blue
HAIR Strawberry blonde
POWERS Cybernetic controls in her costume allowed her to shrink or increase her height at will by using Pym particles. Her costume also enabled her to fly and to fire powerful blasts from her gauntlets.
ALLIES Hank Pym, Vision, Captain Mar-Vell, Guardians of the Galaxy
FOES Iron Man, Immortus

Yellowjacket's strength was much greater in giant form, but growing in size strained her heart.

Activated by thought commands transmitted via her helmet, Rita's Yellowjacket costume enabled her to fly and change size.

She had electric "stingers" in her gloves that packed a powerful punch.

SUPER HERO HANK
The original Yellowjacket, scientist Hank Pym, was a stalwart member of early Avengers teams.

POWER RANK	ENERGY PROJECTION	STRENGTH	DURABILITY	FIGHTING SKILL	INTELLIGENCE	SPEED
	3	5	2	2	2	3

YONDU

Yondu is a member of the Zatoan tribe native to the planet Centauri IV. He met the Super Hero Vance Astro when the Earth astronaut landed on his homeworld shortly before the alien Badoon invaded. Captured by the Badoon, the two escaped and formed the Guardians of the Galaxy to fight against the invaders. As a Guardian, Yondu has helped safeguard the universe. He has also traveled back to the present several times, fighting alongside the Avengers against Korvac.

A splinter group of Yondu's ancestors is linked to the Inhumans. Both races owe their origins to genetic manipulation by the Kree in the distant past.

By emitting a special series of sounds, Yondu can control the path of his arrows.

NATURAL GUARDIAN
Yondu's deep sense of honor and link to nature made him an important member of the Guardians of the Galaxy.

His bow and arrows are made from yaka, a special sound-sensitive metal found only on Centauri IV.

VITAL STATS
REAL NAME Yondu Udonta
OCCUPATION Adventurer
BASE Mobile
HEIGHT Unrevealed
WEIGHT Unrevealed
EYES Unrevealed **HAIR** None
POWERS As a native Centaurian, Yondu has a mystical rapport with many living things, both higher and lower life-forms. He can replenish his strength by communing with nature. He is an expert archer and can make his arrows change direction in mid-flight, or even return to him, by emitting a series of commands.
ALLIES Guardians of the Galaxy, Avengers, Firelord
FOES Badoon, Stark

ENERGY PROJECTION	STRENGTH	DURABILITY	FIGHTING SKILL	INTELLIGENCE	SPEED	POWER RANK
1	4	2	6	3	2	

"AVENGERS ASSEMBLE!"

Senior Editor Alastair Dougall
Project Art Editor Owen Bennett
Design Dynamo Limited
Senior Pre-Production Producer Jennifer Murray
Pre-Production Producer Siu Chan
Senior Producer Alex Bell
Managing Art Editor Maxine Pedliham
Managing Editor Laura Gilbert
Art Director Lisa Lanzarini
Publisher Julie Ferris
Publishing Director Simon Beecroft

First published in the United States in 2010 by
DK Publishing, 345 Hudson Street,
New York, New York 10014
This updated and expanded edition published in 2015.

10 9 8 7 6 5 4 3 2 1
001-270979-March/15

Published in Great Britain by Dorling Kindersley Limited
A Penguin Random House Company

A catalog record for this book is
available from the Library of Congress.

ISBN: 978-1-4654-3001-4

Printed and bound in China by Hung Hing

marvel.com
© 2015 MARVEL

A WORLD OF IDEAS:
SEE ALL THERE IS TO KNOW